Character Structure
and Impulsiveness

PERSONALITY AND PSYCHOPATHOLOGY

A Series of Monographs, Texts, and Treatises

1. The Anatomy of Achievement Motivation, *Heinz Heckhausen.* 1966
2. Cues, Decisions, and Diagnoses: A Systems-Analytic Approach to the Diagnosis of Psychopathology, *Peter E. Nathan.* 1967
3. Human Adaptation and Its Failures, *Leslie Phillips.* 1968
4. Schizophrenia: Research and Theory, *William E. Broen, Jr.* 1968
5. Fears and Phobias, *I. M. Marks.* 1969
6. Language of Emotion, *Joel R. Davitz.* 1969
7. Feelings and Emotions, *Magda Arnold.* 1970
8. Rhythms of Dialogue, *Joseph Jaffe* and *Stanley Feldstein.* 1970
9. Character Structure and Impulsiveness, *David Kipnis.* 1971

In Preparation

The Control of Aggression and Violence: Cognitive and Physiological Factors, *Jerome L. Singer*

Delinquency and Crime: A Biopsychosocial Approach, *Juan B. Cortés and Florence M. Gatti*

CHARACTER STRUCTURE AND IMPULSIVENESS

DAVID KIPNIS

DEPARTMENT OF PSYCHOLOGY
TEMPLE UNIVERSITY
PHILADELPHIA , PENNSYLVANIA

1971

ACADEMIC PRESS   New York and London

ACADEMIC PRESS, INC.
111 Fifth Avenue, New York, New York 10003

United Kingdom Edition published by
ACADEMIC PRESS, INC. (LONDON) LTD.
Berkeley Square House, London W1X 6BA

LIBRARY OF CONGRESS CATALOG CARD NUMBER: 76-127687

PRINTED IN THE UNITED STATES OF AMERICA

Contents

Preface

Understanding the causes of underachievement is of interest from several points of view. At a most general level there is increasing public concern with helping the potential failure to achieve and participate more fully in society. Modestly large sums of money have been invested in programs to achieve this goal, mostly with discouraging results. This lack of success reflects the fact that social scientists have made only minimal progress in understanding the complex interplay among economic forces, cultural influences, and individual strivings, as these influence achievement. One reason for this state of affairs is that each social science discipline views underachievement in terms peculiar to its own level of discourse. As a result, we have parallel explanations of the same event, with no idea how these explanations may be coordinated. For instance, economists view underachievement among poverty groups in terms of a need for guaranteed fixed income, or the lack of same; sociologists view this lack of achievement in terms of subcultural forces; psychologists explain underachievement in terms of intelligence and other personalistic variables. Lacking both a common vocabulary and a common conceptual frame of reference, each discipline must deal with the question at its own level.

Traditionally, psychology has used tests to identify the potential underachiever, and by inference identifies the causes underlying this behavior. No single psychological basis for underachievement has emerged from this research. Anxiety, low levels of intelligence, and lack of achievement motivation are among some of the dimensions identified by tests as related to underachievement. I believe that an important conclusion to be drawn from these findings is that no one method of treatment is liable to elevate the performance of all underachievers. Rather, the potential failure must be helped in terms of the specific psychological deficits revealed by the tests.

This book grew out of my attempt to isolate certain psychological factors that appeared important for the understanding of underachievement among intellectually able adolescents of college age. These bright adolescents had been identified by test score as impulsive.

From the beginning, the goal of this research was to develop procedures to elevate the performance of these adolescents. Initially, however, it was decided to conduct a few simple studies to help understand the kinds of behaviors and attitudes that gave rise to impulsive adolescents' lack of achievement. As I now view this initial decision, I am struck by its naiveté. Each new study revealed further complexities in the behavior of these individuals. What started out as a few simple studies stretched out over a ten-year period, during which time the studies ranged from questions concerned with interpersonal relations to questions of vocational choice. At the same time my views of the impulsive adolescent changed from mild antipathy toward individuals who were not realizing their intellectual potential, to an appreciation of the many strengths, as well as weaknesses, which they manifested.

In retrospect, I realize that my views were unwittingly influenced by the adoption of a model of personality taken from psychopathology. Such a model is necessarily one-sided, emphasizing dysfunctional aspects of behavior. When applied in a normal population, the investigator is guided away from positive aspects of behavior that are also shown by the individual. Fortunately, corrective feedback to this earlier model was provided by experiments in which impulsive persons appeared in a more impressive light than nonimpulsive persons. For example, I was not prepared for the "gauche" behavior of nonimpulsive subjects when interacting with others. Despite these corrections to my original assumptions, it was still possible to realize the primary goal of this research. A final chapter in this monograph describes research which sought to elevate the academic performance of intelligent, but impulsive students. The results of this work support my belief that it is possible to both identify potential underachievers and develop methods of elevating their performances.

As is true with all on-going research, however, the answers to my original questions have only generated new questions which need to be solved. Thus the reader should view this book as an interim report. At this point I am impressed with the wide range of social behaviors in which one may detect the influence of variations in impulsiveness. The implications of these findings from both a practical view and from a concern with personality theory remain to be worked out.

In carrying out the research reported here I am particularly indebted to several colleagues. The leadership study reported in Chapter 5 was done in collaboration with Carl Wagner. The field study reported in Chapter 9, concerned with the elevation of academic performance, was also a collaborative effort with Jerome H. Resnick. I am particularly grateful to Eleanore Isard for providing a professional counseling staff for this study and to Edward Strong for his yeoman service as research assistant during the study. Barry Goodstadt helped plan and supervise the studies on interpersonal relations (Chapter 6) and Leonard Berger gathered the data concerned with the relation between satisfaction and choice of college major (Chapter 8). The criticisms and suggestions offered by Russell Eisenman during the final stages of formulation and writing of this book were exceptionally helpful. Finally, the professional and wifely counsel of Dorothy M. Kipnis is affectionately saluted, from several points of view.

The research reported in Chapter 9 was supported by a grant from the Office of Naval Research. In addition, The Trustees Fund of Temple University provided several small grants at critical times when expenses were mounting too high. I wish to thank the American Psychological Association for permission to reproduce material from articles appearing in the *Journal of Consulting and Clinical Psychology*, the *Journal of Applied Psychology*, the *Journal of Personality and Social Psychology*, and the *Journal of Counseling Psychology*. Finally, I wish to thank Consulting Psychological Press, Inc., for permission to use the Socialization Scale from the California Psychological Inventory.

David Kipnis

**Character Structure
and Impulsiveness**

CHAPTER 1

Introduction

That personality theories are functional in nature is one of the basic generalizations about personality theories offered by Hall and Lindzey in their well-known "Theories of Personality." That is, personality theories are concerned with questions that make a difference in the adjustment of the organism. Why do persons underachieve? Feel happy or depressed? What personality characteristics are associated with creativity? These questions and others like them underlie much of the initial impetus of personality research.

The primary objective of this book stems from the tradition of functionalism. It is concerned with the study of intellectually able individuals who fail in socially defined achievement roles such as are found at school or work. These individuals do not underachieve for lack of ability. Rather, they share a common set of attitudes and behavioral tendencies that are most usually described in terms of character structure. These individuals have been labeled impulsive.

The research described in this book had several broad aims. The first was to study the kinds of behaviors and attitudes that were associated with the construct of impulsiveness, and the way that these behaviors and attitudes contributed to the impulsive individual's lack of achievement. The second aim was to investigate, through laboratory and field studies, the conditions in the environment that influenced the behavior and performance of impulsive persons. That is, under what conditions were impulsive individuals most likely to fail and under what conditions were they most likely to achieve? Thus, in the present research we asked which behaviors define impulsiveness and which environmental settings are most likely to evoke or constrain the expression of these behaviors.

Background

Experimentation documented in this book began with a routine test-validation study in which it was found that adolescents who differed in their self-descriptions on a paper-and-pencil test also differed in their level of achievement at school. In itself, of course, this kind of finding is not unusual. There are literally hundreds of similar results reported each year in psychological journals concerned with psychometrics, education, and testing. What stimulated my interest in this matter was that the self-description–achievement relationship only seemed to occur among more intelligent adolescents. Why should this be? Why didn't the test predict achievement among the less intelligent as well? In an effort to answer this question, I began to examine what these bright underachievers were like and what specifically contributed to their academic difficulties. As the inquiry progressed, it became clear that in order to understand the basis for their underachievement, it would first be necessary to describe the underlying behaviors which gave rise to their underachievement. Looked at in this way, the question of underachievement was seen as embedded in the broader question of variations in behaviors most generally included under the rubric of character development. Thus, the research, which began with questions of test-validation, was eventually broadened to include the kinds of questions outlined in the opening section.

At this point, the reader may anticipate that this book will tell him a good deal about bright underachieving individuals who have been labeled impulsive, but he may wonder whether the results will reveal anything about the general process of character development. Clearly, this is a legitimate concern, since throughout the book I discuss the results as if they did bear on general issues of character structure. In order to speak at this level, I have made several assumptions. The first assumption relates to the structure of personality. I assume that a set of response tendencies relating to character structure cluster together, statistically speaking, to form a fundamental dimension of personality. Included in these response tendencies are responses to affect-laden stimuli, responses to social values, responses to interpersonal influence, and responses to sensory stimulation. Support for this assumption is given in the next section of this chapter which reviews the literature concerned with character development. Next, I have assumed that the paper-and-pencil tests used in our studies at least crudely measure individual differences in this fundamental dimension. Support for this assumption is based upon the fact that persons identified by our tests as impulsive behave in a manner predicted by research using other measures of character development already known and conceptualized in this area. It is reasonable to believe that to the extent that differing measuring instruments converge in their descriptions of behavior, they are measuring overlapping aspects of the same fundamental dimension.

Literature Review

The study of character development has derived its data from many sources. These include clinical and laboratory studies of the institutionalized character-disordered personality, studies of identity crises among troubled adolescents (Erikson, 1959), and psychometric studies that have attempted to delimit the construct of character development from other personality constructs. Despite the diversity of methods and theoretical orientations used, the findings from these approaches tend to converge in their descriptions of the characterologically disturbed person. It is from these areas of agreement that we have taken our starting point. As we have already mentioned, our research has focused upon four areas as being most likely to provide an understanding of how persons classified by test score as impulsive or nonimpulsive differ in behavior. These areas are (1) degree of acceptance of conventional social values; (2) threshholds of responsiveness to anxiety or shame-provoking stimuli; (3) responsiveness to social influence; and (4) responsiveness to sensory stimulation.

What these behaviors have in common is the fact that they all serve as mechanisms through which social controls are applied to the individual. That is, if the individual is for some reason tempted to exhibit some socially prohibited behavior such as aggression, stealing, exploitation, and the like, whether or not he will actually carry out this prohibited behavior will depend upon the restraining influence of one or several of the above forms of control.

First of all, the individual may be restrained by an internalized value system that forbids the action on ethical grounds. Or again, he may be restrained because he does not wish to experience the possible shame accompanying detection or because he experiences anxiety over the punishment he might receive if caught. He may be restrained by the advice and influence of peers or teachers who counsel against the action. Contrarily, the individual may be tempted to carry out the action in order to relieve feelings of tedium and boredom. In this sense, his antisocial behavior may have no other function than to return the individual to a comfortable level of sensory stimulation by seeking excitement (Berlyne, 1960; Quay, 1965).

In the next few pages a brief review is given of the literature relating to these core-restraining behaviors. The reader will observe that most of the literature cited is based upon a comparison of institutionalized character-disordered persons with normals. This is because empirical studies of the normal adolescent in terms of these restraining behaviors are infrequent, with perhaps the exception of Eysenck's (1957) research. Hence, one is required to use the extensive literature on psychopathy and extrapolate from it when developing hypotheses concerning individual differences in impulsiveness within the normal range of the population.

This use of the clinical literature to generate hypotheses about the normal individual requires comment. Basically, we view the psychopath as representing an individual whose behavior is very poorly controlled by the sources of restraint described above. Within the normal range of personality we also expect to find individuals varying in the extent to which these sources of restraint control behavior. Toward the poorly restrained end we have placed the impulsive individual, whose behavior should mirror, with lesser intensity, the behavior of the psychopath. This view is similar to Eysenck's description of the dimension of introversion–extroversion (1957). At one end of his dimension he has placed the quiet, well-socialized, overly controlled, conventional, and rather shy introvert, and toward the other end the unconventional, noisy, hail-fellow-well-met, somewhat untrustworthy, extrovert. It is pertinent to point out that Eysenck considers the psychopath to be a highly extroverted individual. Thus, at the extreme he has placed the unconcerned, exploitive, asocial, and thrill-seeking psychopath. From this view, one may then make comparisons between the psychopath and normals (which includes introverts and extroverts) or comparisons between introverts and extroverts within the normal range of personality. If we are dealing with a true continuum, both comparisons should yield similar findings. Furthermore, facts discovered about the psychopath should also hold for the extrovert, although with less dramatic intensity.

REACTIONS TO NEGATIVE AFFECTIVE STIMULI

The first source of restraint we wish to examine is concerned with the person's own reactions to his impulsive behavior, that is, the extent to which the person inhibits a momentary urge because of accompanying feelings of shame or anxiety. Within a normal population these kinds of feelings are often mentioned as the reason for restraining one's impulses. Such reasons are less frequently mentioned, however, by character-disordered individuals. Indeed, Cleckley (1941) and Karpman (1948), among others, believe that the psychopath's frequently noted failure to learn from past experience, in the sense of "once burned, twice wary," is due to the fact that negative affective states are only fleetingly experienced by this group. As a result, psychopaths are not inhibited by these restraining emotions when contemplating some antisocial act. Although it is difficult to describe in a few brief paragraphs the wide range of studies that have addressed themselves to the question of emotional reactivity among psychopaths, perhaps a study of Hare's (1965) adequately illustrates these concerns. In this study, Hare was concerned with obtaining information on physiological and emotional differences between psychopaths and normals in their reactions to an oncoming electric shock. In essence, Hare asked whether normals and psychopaths differed in their emotional anticipations of an event that was liable to hurt them.

Subjects were penitentiary inmates classified as psychopathic or nonpsychopathic who had been told beforehand that they would receive an intense electric shock when the number eight appeared in front of them. Skin conductance, as a measure of emotional arousal, was monitored for each subject while the numbers from 1 to 12 were consecutively presented on a moving tape. As the count approached the number eight, the increase in skin conductance (or emotional arousal) was smaller and less rapid and began later for the psychopath than for the nonpsychopath. As Hare says, "it is tempting to suggest here that the psychopath's short-range hedonism, poor judgment, and lack of impulse control may be related to the fact that the aversive aspects of a threatened punishment do not become apparent until the punishment is very close in time" (page 18, 1965). In other words, Hare is suggesting that the restraining controls exercised by emotions are weaker and occur too late to be effective among psychopaths. In addition, data are presented in Chapter 4 that suggest that there may be fewer situations capable of arousing negative affect among persons with this basic character structure.

SENSATION SEEKING

The second source of restraint that can inhibit impulsive behavior arises from the strength of the individual's need for social stimulation and excitement. Restlessness and feelings of boredom are strong goads to activity. Several theorists have proposed that too little sensory stimulation produces psychological discomfort as unpleasant as that produced by anxiety, for example. Hence, understimulation may act as a drive state impelling the individual to seek out stimulation. Furthermore, it has been proposed that there is an optimal level of excitation that produces psychological comfort (Berlyne, 1960). Not all persons, of course, may require the same optimal level of excitation. Zuckerman and his co-workers (1964; 1968) have presented evidence that individuals differ widely in how much stimulation they seek from the environment as a means of maintaining this optimal level.

The relevance of these individual differences in sensation seeking for the present research is that many clinicians have commented that the psychopath seems unable to tolerate routine and boredom. Quay (1965) has written that the psychopath's penchant for creating excitement, his antisocial, even vicious, behaviors and his outbursts frequently appear to be motivated by little more than a need for thrills and excitement. Quay and others (Eysenck, 1967; Hare, 1968) have hypothesized that the psychopath is in a chronic state of cortical underarousal and that he attempts to increase arousal to some more optimal level by seeking stimulation in the form of excitement and thrill seeking. Furthermore, a related hypothesis is that the psychopath requires a greater amount of stimulation to obtain an optimal level of arousal.

Given the elegance of the theory, the experimental studies to test these related hypotheses are limited. However, there is some evidence that extroverts tend to satiate more rapidly on various perceptual-motor-type tasks (Eysenck, 1957) and weak evidence that persons with high *Pd* (psychopathic deviate) and *Ma* (manic) scores on the MMPI (Minnesota Multi-phasic Inventory) do not make satisfactory adjustments to a sensory deprivation environment (Zubeck, 1969). Other evidence on the need for sensory stimulation comes from studies of time estimation in which it has been reported that character-disordered persons overestimated the duration of unfilled time more frequently than normal controls (Orme, 1962; Siegman, 1961). That is, for character-disordered persons, when required to just sit and do nothing, time seemed to pass far more slowly than it did for normals.

ACCEPTANCE OF CONVENTIONAL VALUES

This area needs little comment insofar as it relates to the inhibition of behavior. In American society the values stressed are those that reward ambition, achievement, success, self-control, respect for property, and the like. Many of these values are specifically concerned with self-regulation of behavior, as for example, "be a good sport," "obey the rules," "don't cheat," "do your best," and the like. To the extent that the individual comes to believe in the importance of these regulative values, he will tend to inhibit behaviors that violate these beliefs. Most authors agree that characterologically retarded individuals have not internalized these regulatory values (Loevinger, 1966; McCord, McCord, and Zola, 1959). In describing persons retarded in ego development Loevinger states that "rules are not recognized as such; an action is bad because it is punished. Morality is purely an expedient one. What is bad is to be caught (page 199)." In other words, internalized restraining forces likely to inhibit impulsive behaviors exert only minimal influence among characterologically disturbed persons.

SOCIAL INFLUENCE

The influence of other persons constitutes a fourth source liable to restrain behavior. Clinical observations suggest that psychopaths are less influenced by peers and authority figures than are normals. That is, once instigated to achieve some desired goal, attempts to change the psychopath's behavior through the use of praise, criticism, suggestions, and advice are more frequently ignored by psychopaths than by normals. Along these lines it is well known that character-disordered personalities are poor risks in therapy because of their antagonism and conflicts concerning close interpersonal relations (Thorne, 1959) and their lack of motivation to even seek out therapeutic help (Schwitzgebel, 1969).

Experimental attempts to confirm these clinical observations have yielded mixed results. In these studies, character-disordered persons and normals have been given tasks that have either alternate solutions (mainly verbal conditioning tasks), or are difficult and require assistance. The goal of the experimenter is to switch subjects from their initially preferred method of performing the task through praising the alternate method, or criticizing subjects' preferred method. The experimenter may also be interested in whether subjects ask for help. As we have said, the results of these studies are mixed. In some instances psychopaths resist influence from the experimenter as predicted (Cairns, 1961; Hetherington and Klinger, 1964; Johns and Quay, 1962; Sarbin, Allen and Rutherford, 1965). In other instances psychopaths accept the advice and praise of the experimenter and change their behavior (Bernard and Eisenman, 1967; Bryan and Kapche, 1967; Persons, 1968). Apparently the dimensions underlying this process of influence have not been adequately conceptualized. For example, Stewart and Resnick (1970) reported that psychopathic persons showed verbal conditioning when the subject and the experimenter were of opposite sex, but not when they were of the same sex. Other unexamined characteristics of the experimenter and the situation may also account for these mixed results, such as, for example, the experimenter's personal warmth or his status in relation to the subject. Since this area of research is particularly vulnerable to experimental errors related to the demand characteristics of verbal conditioning tasks, as well as to errors arising from the experimenter's expectancies, greater efforts to control these sources of bias may have to be made. At this point we may conclude that although the weight of clinical evidence supports the assertion that psychopaths are less open to influence from others, experimental evidence to support this assertion remains weak.

THE INFLUENCE OF MATERIAL REWARDS

Since the behavior of the psychopath is poorly restrained by feelings of psychic distress, social approval or disapproval, low levels of sensory inputs, intrinsic rewards resulting from the expectation of accomplishing long-range goals, and by the acceptance of conventional social values, the question arises as to whether there exists any class of incentives which do have enough reinforcing strength to modify the character-disordered person's behavior. One class of incentive that has been mentioned in the literature as exerting some control is the awarding or withholding of material incentives. Since material rewards were used in our research as a means of influencing the behavior of impulsive individuals, we will briefly review the literature that suggested the importance of the reward factor.

One of the earlier reports in this regard was based upon the long-term studies of behavior-disordered children by Levine and Spivack (1959). These authors reported that in a residential treatment setting, the conforming behavior of these children was markedly influenced by the frequency of weekend privileges. When the privileges were suspended temporarily, conformity decreased, despite the maintenance of a long-range reward program of value to the boys. Tyler (1965) also found that an acting-out delinquent's academic performance could be modified by reinforcing his academic efforts and performance with tokens exchangeable for privileges and canteen items. Every day after school the boy was awarded tokens for his academic efforts, based upon a grade sheet filled in by his teachers. For the four semesters preceding the study, in which the boy received intensive counseling and standard therapeutic treatment, his grade-point averages had been .60, 1.00, .50, and 1.20. During the 30 weeks of the study his grade-point average rose to 3.00. Most recently, Schwitzgebel (1969) demonstrated that offering small amounts of money to delinquents motivated them to attend therapy sessions. Presumably the money served as a substitute for psychic distress, the usual basis for motivating persons to attend therapy.

Schmauk (1968) in an extension of Lykken's well-known study of avoidance learning among psychopathic prisoners also found evidence of this group's overvaluation of money and material objects. In Schmauk's study, psychopaths were either verbally criticized for making a wrong response on a mental maze learning task, were electrically shocked, or were deprived of money they had initially been given. As in Lykken's original study, the psychopathic group failed to learn the avoidance response when shock was used. Similarly, no avoidance learning was found when they were criticized. However, when the psychopaths were threatened with loss of money, they learned the avoidance response as well as a control group. Thus, the threat of loss of money served to facilitate the learning of new behaviors which both tangible punishment and verbal criticisms were unable to do.

Finally, Thorne (1959), in a long article discussing his therapeutic experiences with psychopathic patients, also came to the conclusion that one could alter their behavior through the use of money. In essence, Thorne proposed that the therapists be made what amounts to the financial guardian of the psychopathic patient. Through manipulation of the amounts of money given the patient, Thorne believed that the therapist could induce the psychopath to be more responsive to the actual therapeutic sessions.

Taken together, then, these studies suggested to us the importance of money and material rewards and provided the rationale for using this form of incentive among our impulsive subjects.

Summary and Overview

From the literature concerned with character structure and character disorder, we have selected four aspects of behavior that seem likely to underlie differences in the academic achievement of impulsive and non-impulsive persons. The behaviors selected represent differing modes of controlling impulsive behavior; this book is primarily concerned with exploring the ways in which these controls serve to inhibit and facilitate behavior.

Chapter 2 describes in more detail the paper-and-pencil tests used to measure impulsiveness. Chapter 3 presents the relationship between these tests and achievement at school and at work. The findings from these studies indicated that the tests could identify with modest accuracy those individuals who were most likely to fail or underachieve. An important discovery made in these early studies was that intellectual ability mediated the relationship between impulsiveness and achievement. It was mainly among the more intelligent segments of each sample studied that impulsiveness predicted achievement. Among less intelligent segments, level of impulsiveness was not predictive of achievement. While the reasons underlying these findings remain unclear, a search of the literature did reveal that upon occasion, other investigators had also reported similar findings. Most immediately, this finding was used to more precisely identify those impulsive individuals who were likely to underachieve.

Why should intelligent (but impulsive) persons fail? What kinds of attitudes typified their approach to achievement? This book addresses itself to these kinds of questions. Chapters 4 through 7 present a series of studies concerned with the relationship between impulsiveness, as defined by test scores, and measures of the several response dimensions outlined in the preceding pages. Chapter 8 presents data as to how these core behaviors are manifested in occupational interest and career intentions. Some of the findings to be reported in these chapters, such as those in the area of self-control, acceptance of conventional values, and affective reactions have been well documented by others. These findings are of interest insofar as they suggest the construct validity of our measuring instruments. More importantly, they are of interest because they find that many of the behaviors and attitudes commonly associated with institutionalized psychopaths may also be detected within the normal range of population among persons classified as impulsive. Other findings in these chapters concerning relationships with friends and vocational choice have not been well explored. These latter findings provide new and sometimes perplexing insights into the meaning of impulsiveness and character development within the normal population.

In addition to the study of correlates of impulsiveness, Chapters 4 through 7 are concerned with the identification of environmental factors that may influence the behavior of impulsive and nonimpulsive individuals. The results of these studies suggest the importance of money as an incentive. In addition, the results suggest the influence of clearly imposed environmental restraints in inhibiting impulsiveness. Finally, in Chapter 9, a single long-term field study is reported that attempted to use the previously gathered information to elevate the school performance of intelligent but impulsive college students.

CHAPTER 2

Measurement of Impulsiveness

We can assess an individual's level of character development through several methods, the most complex of which is based upon the clinical judgment of a psychiatrist or psychologist who seeks to integrate information from interviews, case history materials, and psychological tests. In contrast, a second method is rather simple and is based on whether or not the individual has been in prison. The assumption is that individuals who repeatedly violate society's norms and laws are by definition character-disordered. Finally, paper-and-pencil tests have been used alone or in combination with other devices to measure character development. Strictly speaking, these latter devices have been developed not only to distinguish the character-disordered from the normal, but also to measure variations in character development within the normal range of population.

All of the above methods have their strengths and weaknesses. Clinical judgments provide elaborate insights into the dynamics that underlie each individual case. However, the clinician must spend a good deal of time and effort in arriving at these judgments and hence this procedure cannot be used for large-scale research measurements. Furthermore, despite the time and effort expended, clinicians frequently do not agree with each other in their diagnosis, which makes this measurement procedure somewhat unreliable. Whether or not a person has been imprisoned allows for clear-cut criterion comparisons with nonimprisoned controls, but has the drawback that prison populations tend to be somewhat heterogeneous in personality makeup (Panton, 1960). Aside from violating society's laws, prisoners may differ almost as much among themselves in personality as do nonprisoners. Paper-and-pencil tests allow one to study larger and more representative samples of the population, although at the expense of the in-depth information provided by clinical assessment or clear-cut differentiation provided by criterion group analysis.

As was stated in Chapter 1, the classification of subjects in our research was based upon paper-and-pencil tests. In this chapter we will describe these tests and the reasons for their use. Included in these descriptions is evidence for the construct validity of our tests, including their relations with the other two modes of measuring character development—clinical judgments and imprisonment.

Initially, a paper-and-pencil biographical scale (called the Impulsiveness Scale*) was used as the sole measure of impulsiveness. As the research progressed, however, it was felt desirable to strengthen our measurement procedures by using several scales in combination. Accordingly, scores from the Socialization Scale of the California Psychological Inventory (CPI) were combined with the first scale to form an index of impulsiveness. Combining the two scales in this way, assumes that a fundamental dimension of personality exists to be measured (this point has already been discussed in Chapter 1), and that the Impulsiveness Scale and the Socialization Scale are measuring differing aspects of the same basic dimension. If they are not, combining the scores would lead to meaningless results. In a sample of 573 male university students the two scales intercorrelated .45, suggesting a modest overlap in measurement between the two scales. Another way of examining whether the scales are measuring the same dimension is to see if they both predict behavior in the same manner. If we consistently find that one scale predicts a given behavior, say reaction to anxiety-provoking stimuli, while the second scale does not predict, or worse, predicts in an opposite direction, then it can be concluded that combining scales will not yield superior measurement of the dimension of behavior under study.

In all instances where we have examined the direction of prediction, it has been found that the dependent measures under study were predicted in the same direction and at relatively the same magnitude by each scale, when considered alone. In many instances, combining scale scores yielded slightly stronger relations with the dependent measures than either scale by itself (Kipnis, 1968b; Steward and Resnick, in press).

The Impulsiveness Index was obtained by simply adding the unweighted

---

* This scale was originally called the Insolence Scale in previous publications. For ease of discussion the scale has been retitled as the Impulsiveness Scale.

scores of the two scales together. Since the standard deviations of both scales were almost exactly equal, both scales contributed equal weight to the combined Impulsiveness Index. In the research that follows, unless otherwise indicated, persons with top-third scores on the Impulsiveness Scale or Impulsiveness Index were designated as impulsive, while persons with bottom-third scores were designated as nonimpulsive.

Development of the Impulsiveness Scale

The development of this scale originated in a Navy project to develop measures that would predict enlisted men's school and job performance (Kipnis and Glickman, 1962). Among the tests included in this research was the Risk Scale, developed by Torrance and Ziller (1957). The Risk Scale had been developed in an attempt to identify individuals who might succeed in risky occupations. The scale consisted of 58 biographical-type items concerned with the individual's participation as a child, and currently in various social and sports events. The scale also included questions on the respondent's leadership behaviors, his relations with school authorities, and with parents.

Torrance and Ziller had based the scale upon interviews with pilots during the Korean War who were either aces or non-aces. Aces had shot down at least five enemy planes. In validation studies, Torrance and Ziller found that persons with high scores on the Risk Scale tended to perform at superior levels in dangerous types of occupations. In other words, individuals who succeeded in risky occupations had an early history that systematically differed from less successful individuals in risky occupations. Parenthetically, Torrance and Ziller found that a fair number of the successful combat pilots made very poor garrison soldiers. These high risk-takers had great difficulty in accepting orders from their superior officers.

In our first Risk Scale tryout we found a negative relationship between the scale and supervisors' ratings of the job proficiency of a sample of enlisted men. Seeking clarification, the Risk Scale was item-analyzed against this rating of performance criterion. It was found that men who were considered unsatisfactory by their supervisors described themselves on the Risk Scale as having started at an early age to drink, smoke, gamble, dance, have an interest in sex, hitchhike, and take overnight trips without their family. They were more likely to take dares and to report doing cruel things as a child, and were punished for bad conduct in school. They enjoyed swimming and the types of sports that involved bodily contact. In general, the self-descriptions portrayed physically active, aggressive, somewhat reckless personalities. From the negative validities of the first study, we suspected that the high risk-takers maintained an independent and rebellious attitude toward most attempts by authority to control their behavior.

The 27 discriminating items from the Risk Scale were incorporated into a separate scoring key. In a new study, these 27 items yielded higher validities against supervisors' evaluations of performance than scores from the total Risk Scale, suggesting that this subset of items carried the major burden of prediction. Next, additional items describing aspects of childhood and adult activities, similar to the first 27 items were added to the 27-item key, yielding a final 41-item scale. Despite the empirical nature of the item selection, the items clearly reveal a developmental basis for the current behavior of respondents, in terms of poor relations with school authority and early interest in thrill seeking, and in such social activities as sex and drinking. The scale is homogeneous in makeup, as indicated by a split-half reliability of .84 computed among 222 university students. Appendix 1 presents the scale items and scoring key.

Evidence on the construct validity of the scale is presented throughout the book in terms of its relations with behaviors usually considered to define the dimension of impulsiveness. In addition to these relations, correlations between the Impulsiveness Scale and other test measures of character structure are as follows: .41 with the Extroversion Scale of the Maudsley Personality Scale, $-.41$ with the Achiever Personality Scale of Fricke's Opinion, Attitude and Interest Survey $-.18$ with the TAT measure of need achievement, .45 with the Socialization Scale of the California Psychological Inventory, .25 with the *Ma* Scale from the MMPI, and .09 with the Neuroticism Scale of the Maudsley Personality Inventory. In two separate studies the Impulsiveness Scale correlated .29 and .53 with the *Pd* Scale from the MMPI. This latter correlation is probably inflated by the fact that half the sample was taken from a delinquent home and half from a public high school.

Stewart and Resnick (in press) have found that 90% of a group of institutionalized delinquents had high-third Impulsiveness Scale scores while only 30% of a control sample had high-third scores ($r_{bis} = .76, p < .01$), suggesting that the scale is a measure of the tendency to commit antisocial forms of behavior. The scale also correlated .66 with psychiatrists' diagnoses of psychopathic personality among a sample of incoming psychiatric patients at the Bethesda Naval Hospital (Kipnis, 1965a). This correlation was found only among patients with average or better intelligence scores, suggesting that the scale's validity is moderated by intelligence.

In other correlational studies the Impulsiveness Scale did not correlate with age or response set as measured by the Set for True Scale ($r = .18$) and the Infrequent Response Scale ($r = .01$) of Fricke's OAIS, or social desirability as measured by the Marlow–Crowne Social Desirability Scale ($r = .05$). Correlations between the Impulsiveness Scale and estimates of intelligence based upon the navy's General Classification Test and the Scholastic Aptitude Test have consistently been zero. Other test relations will be given in subsequent parts of the book.

The Socialization Scale

This is a 51-item true–false attitude scale from the California Psychological Inventory.* This scale was included with the Impulsiveness Scale in several of the latter studies among college samples. Gough (1965) has described the scale as able to identify individuals along a continuum of asocial to social behavior and as able to forecast the likelihood that any individual will violate the rules and norms of his culture. This scale has been extensively validated as a measure of antisocial tendencies. Results of a wide variety of studies, summarized by Gough (1965) indicate that persons described as asocial by the scale do indeed exhibit such behaviors as delinquency, underachievement in school, violation of parole, and a lack of responsiveness to social reinforcement. In the *Annual Review of Psychology* Adelson (1969) described the Socialization Scale as one of the best measures for determining antisocial behaviors.

The Use of Tests

Underlying the research in this book are certain assumptions about the use of psychological tests which it is appropriate to discuss here. One of the main uses of tests in our society has been to eliminate from institutional enrollment individuals identified as likely to fail. Both in universities and in industry, tests have been used in this manner to improve the functioning of the organization, by rejecting the potential failure. Unfortunately, this usage has increasingly revealed itself as divisive and instrumental in maintaining inequities in our society by systematically eliminating disadvantaged minority group applicants. There is perhaps an apocryphal story about how psychological tests lost the Belgian Congo for Belgium, that is appropriate here. It seems that the Belgian colonists were sensitive to the charge that they were systematically excluding black congolese from participation in industry and government. To avoid further charges of favoritism and racism, the Belgian government instituted a psychological testing program, which all applicants, white or black, had to pass in order to be hired. Most

* Three items were omitted as being inappropriate for a college population.

persons would consider this an eminently fair procedure that allowed all an equal opportunity. Unfortunately none of the black congolese were able to exceed the tests' cutting scores. Surprisingly and despite the fairness of the procedures now instituted, the black congolese instituted a series of revolts that culminated in the return of the white colonists to Belgium, tests and all.

When used for screening purposes tests are in fact diagnostic instruments. They provide information about the psychological disabilities of an individual that may impede his performance. In this regard it is instructive to examine how the more advanced field of medical diagnostics uses its diagnostic devices. This comparison is shown in Table 1.

TABLE 1

COMPARISON OF THE USE OF PSYCHOLOGICAL AND MEDICAL DIAGNOSTIC INSTRUMENTS

Steps in development and use of diagnostic instrument	Medicine	Psychology
1. Past research, hunches, or theory used as the basis for development of instrument	Yes	Yes
2. Validation—empirical demonstrations that instrument maximally differentiates either sick from well or successful from unsuccessful; test validity maximized	Yes	Yes
3. If person has critical score, steps taken to cure	Yes; therapy begun if possible	No; information used to eliminate person
4. Evaluation of therapy by readministering diagnostic device; success measured by device no longer distinguishing sick person from well; test validity reduced to zero	Yes	No

It can be seen that a major difference between the two disciplines is that medicine uses its diagnostic information to treat and perhaps cure the patient. If the treatment is successful, a subsequent application of the diagnostic instrument no longer differentiates between the sick and the well. Applied psychology contrarily uses its diagnostic information to eliminate the sick. Where they go, no one knows—perhaps to the Congo.

From this brief comparison with medicine, I would suggest that a more inclusive goal for applied uses of psychological tests might be to first maximize test validity as a means of identifying the particular psychological disability that leads to failure in a given situation. Second, steps should be instituted to improve the performance of low test scorers. An interesting consequence of these steps, if successful, will be to reduce test validity back down to zero, a goal usually not mentioned in applied textbooks. Nevertheless, such a reduction in test validity could be taken as a sign that the remedial program has achieved its aims, in that low test scorers now perform at the same level as high test scorers.

The above view of the use of psychological tests had an important influence in guiding the research reported in the third section of this book. Given an instrument that identified potential failures, and given information on the causes of this failure, our research attention turned to possible ways to elevate these potential failures using the accumulated information. Our aspirations were perhaps somewhat higher than the obtained results. Nevertheless, the findings as reported in Chapter 9 appeared sufficiently encouraging to suggest the value of using test scores as diagnostic instruments that suggest subsequent treatment.

CHAPTER 3

Performance in Socially Defined Achievement Roles

One of the first demands placed upon teenagers by society is that they master a vocational role, either through formal school training or as an apprentice on-the-job. It appears critical that the completion of this training occur during the individual's late teens or early twenties. After a person has married and assumed obligations for supporting himself and a family, it is difficult to reassume the role of a student. There are, of course, many reasons for not completing occupational training. These may range from poor health, to lack of money, to lack of adequate facilities for training, to lack of motivation, ability, or interest. It is with these latter psychological variables that this chapter is concerned.

Presented in this chapter are several studies on the relation between impulsiveness and performance in training schools or in a training status on-the-job. As was previously mentioned, impulsiveness was found most predictive of performance among persons who were average or better in intellectual ability. Accordingly, in the studies that follow, each sample has been subdivided into several levels of intellectual ability. For the navy samples, the General Classification Test (GCT) a measure of general verbal ability, was used to estimate intelligence. For the college samples, the combined verbal and numerical scores from the Scholastic Aptitude Test (SAT) were used.

Moderator Variables

Before presenting the findings, some discussion is in order concerning the reason intelligence was used to subdivide the samples of persons studied.

Initially, the possibility that improved prediction of behavior using personality tests could be obtained by dividing respondents into subgroups was suggested by the research of Frederiksen and Melville (1954). These authors reported that the validity of a test measuring engineering interest could be improved by eliminating from the overall analysis those persons who were low in compulsiveness, as measured by a second test. Subsequently, Saunders (1956) called this second test, used to eliminate persons from the overall analysis, a moderator variable. The reader is referred to articles by Ghesseli (1963) and Dunnette (1963) for an extensive treatment of this approach to test validity.

In the late 1950's and early 1960's Albert Glickman and I were attempting to develop tests to predict the training school and job performance of Navy enlisted men (Kipnis and Glickman, 1962). One of the tests was a measure of endurance under moderately stressful conditions (produced by the use of a fatiguing motor task). In several studies, endurance was found to correlate with performance at a low, but significant level. Stimulated by Frederiksen and Melville's findings, the endurance data were reanalyzed using intellectual ability as the moderator variable. Somewhat to our surprise, it was found that endurance predicted performance among less intelligent sailors, but not among more intelligent sailors. That is, among sailors with below-average intelligence scores, those with high-endurance test scores outperformed, at school and on the job, sailors with low endurance scores. Among sailors with average or better intelligence scores, endurance was not related to performance (Kipnis, 1962; Kipnis, 1965a; Kipnis and Wagner, 1965a, b). In passing, we may note that these findings are similar to those reported by Stagner (1933)* and by Katahn (1966). These authors also found that measures of reactivity to stress and endurance were differentially predictive of school performance as a function of levels of ability.

In any case, the above findings raised the possibility that intelligence might also moderate impulsiveness. The analyses reported in this chapter directly investigated this possibility.

Prediction of Performance

RADIO SCHOOL PERFORMANCE

In 1957, the Impulsiveness Scale was administered to two classes of navy recruits (N = 134) who had entered a school for the training of telegraphers. The original 27-item scoring key was used in this study. Fourteen months

---

* More precisely, Stagner used the reactivity measure as the moderator variable and found that intelligence predicted grades at higher levels among less reactive students.

after the initial testing, a letter was sent to the supervisor of each sailor asking him to evaluate the sailor on five traits: Willingness to Work; Technical Competence; Respect for Authority; Ability to get along with Shipmates; and Overall Acceptability. These performance evaluations were summed to obtain a criterion score for each sailor. In addition to the job performance information, radio school performance was obtained for each sailor in terms of his proficiency in sending and receiving radio code (words per minute) by the middle of the school term.

In turn, for each criterion, sailors were divided into two groups consisting of those in the bottom third of the criterion distribution (Below Average) and those in the upper two-thirds (Average or Better). The sailors were further subdivided at the median of their GCT scores into those with high intellectual ability and those with low intellectual ability. Finally, at each level of ability, biserial correlations were computed between the impulsiveness scores and the dichotomized criteria. These validity coefficients are shown in Table 2.

TABLE 2

BISERIAL CORRELATIONS BETWEEN THE IMPULSIVENESS SCALE AND
SCHOOL–JOB PERFORMANCE

Subject	Radio school		Job performance[a]	
	r_{bis}	(N)	r_{bis}	(N)
Low-ability sailors	.01	68	−.17	62
High-ability sailors	−.35[b]	66	−.47[c]	61
All cases	−.16	134	−.28[b]	123

[a] Eleven subjects lost through discharge or no response from supervisors.
[b] $p < .05$
[c] $p < .01$

It may be seen that intelligent, but impulsive sailors did more poorly at school and on the job than equally intelligent, nonimpulsive sailors. However, for sailors with lower levels of intelligence, impulsiveness did not predict future performance.

ATTEMPTS TO GENERALIZE

A second large-scale study was done in an attempt to determine whether the above results could be generalized. Samples of navy recruits about to enter each of six navy trade schools were tested with the Impulsiveness Scale (27-item key). Approximately $1\frac{1}{2}$ years later, evaluations of their performance were obtained from each sailor's supervisor. Evaluations of performance were given by the supervisors using four 14-point scales as follows: Technical Competence; Willingness to Work; Respect for Authority; and Overall Evaluation. Each sailor's final grade at trade school was also obtained.

The following vocational areas were represented: Electrician's Mate (EM); Radiomen (RM); Fire Control Technician (FT); Hospital Corpsmen (HM); Interior Communications Specialist (IC); and Machinist Mates (MM).

The analysis was similar to that used in the first study. For final grades at trade school and for each of the four job-performance areas that were evaluated, sailors were split into two groups, consisting of those with

TABLE 3

BISERIAL CORRELATIONS OF THE IMPULSIVENESS SCALE WITH JOB PERFORMANCE[a]

GCT quartile	Samples					
	IC	EM	MM	RM	HM	FT
	Evaluation of Technical Competence					
1–24	.26	.04	.24	−.05	−.24	−.08
25–49	−.12	−.16	−.13	−.08	−.31[b]	−.06
50–74	−.06	−.21	−.07	−.07	−.24	−.13
75–100	−.01	−.20	−.30[b]	−.01	−.24	.03
	Evaluation of Willingness to Work					
1–24	−.02	−.02	.26	−.18	−.09	−.09
25–49	−.16	−.03	.07	−.13	−.38[c]	−.04
50–74	.04	−.18	.11	−.24*	−.31[b]	−.15
75–100	.03	−.18	−.20	−.01	−.31[b]	−.03
	Evaluation of Respect for Authority					
1–24	−.06	.01	.22	−.14	−.21	−.27[b]
25–49	−.08	−.09	−.06	−.07	−.46[c]	−.34[b]
50–74	−.11	−.35[c]	.03	−.30[b]	−.22	−.25[b]
75–100	−.09	−.12	−.33[b]	−.26[b]	−.26[b]	−.07
	Evaluation of Overall Worth					
1–24	.15	.13	.36[b]	−.05	−.09	−.12
25–49	−.17	−.13	.09	.00	−.34[b]	−.13
50–74	.03	−.31[c]	−.05	−.16	−.26[b]	−.06
75–100	−.16	−.22	−.28[b]	−.22	−.33[b]	−.03

[a] By GCT quartiles.
[b] $P < .05$.
[c] $p < .01$.

bottom-third criterion scores and those with scores in the upper two-thirds. Sailors were also subdivided into four quartiles based upon the distribution of GCT scores within each vocational area (from 80 to 90 sailors in each GCT quartile). To estimate the relationship between impulsiveness and performance, biserial correlations were computed between the Impulsiveness Scale and the dichotomized criteria, at each level of GCT.

It was found that impulsiveness did not predict school grades beyond chance level. However, impulsiveness did predict job performance evaluations beyond chance expectancy. Furthermore, prediction was mainly restricted to higher-ability sailors.

As shown in Table 3, of the 20 significant negative validity coefficients, one was found in the lowest GCT quartile, five in the 26th to 50th quartile, and seven in each of the two highest quartiles. Finally, there was a significant positive correlation of .36 ($p < .05$) among MM's in the lowest GCT quartile. This latter correlation suggests the possibility that in some circumstances the combination of *below* average intelligence and impulsiveness may actually facilitate performance.

The construct validity of the scale was supported in the present study by the finding that impulsiveness most clearly predicted evaluations of Respect for Authority and Overall Evaluations. Of the 21 significant correlations, nine were correlated with Respect for Authority and six with Overall Evaluations. The fewest were with Technical Competence, suggesting that intelligent and impulsive sailors encountered their major difficulties in personal interactions with authority figures, rather than in actual ability to do the work.

POSTDICTION OF HIGH SCHOOL GRADUATION

Next, the Impulsiveness Scale (41-item key) was administered to a sample of 193 navy recruits and the attempt was made to postdict whether the recruit had graduated from high school prior to joining the navy. This criterion was used since it reflects one of the first demands placed upon teenagers by society. Failure to complete high school is generally acknowledged to have increasingly serious consequences for subsequent vocational adjustment and success. Hathaway, Reynolds, and Monachesi (1969) have published data on the vocational careers of high school graduates and dropouts that dramatically illustrate the negative outcomes associated with high school failure.

Of the sample, 28% stated that they had not completed high school and were classified as dropouts. Since the navy adopts a selective policy toward the enlistment of men in terms of their intelligence and educational attainment, it is doubtful that the sample used here was representative of high school dropouts throughout the country. Doubt as to the representative nature of the sample is based upon the finding that the correlation between intelligence (GCT) and the dropout–graduate criterion was zero in this sample. Several studies have reported that a moderate to strong correlation exists between intelligence and the successful completion of high school (Cook, 1956; Dresher, 1954). Presumably, the lack of correlation found here reflects the navy's recruiting policy of not encouraging applications from persons with low GCT scores, who also failed to complete high school.

The sample was split into above and below average ability groupings, based upon a median GCT split of 53. Within each ability grouping, biserial correlations were computed between impulsiveness scores and the criterion of dropout versus graduates from high school.

TABLE 4

POSTDICTION OF HIGH SCHOOL GRADUATION
WITH THE IMPULSIVE STATE

Ability	r^{bis}	N
High	$-.60^a$	94
Low	$-.38^a$	99

[a] $p < .01$.

As shown in Table 4, the correlation between the Impulsive Scale and graduation from high school was higher among more intelligent recruits than among less intelligent. The difference between the correlations of $-.60$ and $-.38$ was significant beyond the .05 level, using Fisher's z' transformation.

To determine if there were consistent rises in correlations as intelligence increased, the recruits were subdivided into six GCT levels and biserial correlations were computed between the Impulsiveness Scale and the dropout–graduate criterion, within each GCT grouping. Figure 1 (page 28) shows these correlations, plotted as a function of GCT level. It can be observed that there was a general trend for the correlations to rise, as the intelligence level of the group rose.

Whether or not the Impulsiveness Scale would be predictive of high school dropouts cannot, of course, be determined from the present data. It is quite possible that the very experience of dropping out of high school helped form the kind of character structure indicated by these test scores. Further one would guess that if impulsiveness were predictive of dropouts, the magnitude of the correlations would not be as high as those obtained through postdiction. The experience of psychological measurement is that the "half-life" of a high-validity coefficient is very short indeed.

IMPULSIVENESS AND COLLEGE ACHIEVEMENT

Previous studies used an enlisted military population. In the next study, in collaboration with the late Dr. Gorham Lane, an attempt was made to extend these findings on achievement and impulsiveness to a nonmilitary population of college students. To this end, the entire entering male freshman class (N = 624) at the University of Delaware took the impulsiveness measure (41-item key) prior to the beginning of their freshman year.

The class was divided into three relatively equal groups on the basis of their impulsiveness scores. Students with upper-third scores of 21 or more were designated as impulsive, those with middle-third scores (20 to 16) as moderate impulsive, and those with lower-third scores (15 or less) as nonimpulsiveness. Combined verbal and mathematics scores from the SAT were used as the measure of intellectual ability. Based upon a median SAT score of 1100, students were divided into two relatively equal groups.

Table 5 shows the first-semester final grades of students, jointly classified by impulsiveness and SAT scores. An analysis of variance of these grades yielded a significant interaction between impulsiveness and SAT scores ($F = 3.57$, df 2/612, $p < .05$). Separate analyses within each ability level revealed that impulsiveness predicted grades among students with above average SAT scores ($F = 7.22$, df 2/315, $p < .01$), but did not predict grades among students with below average SAT scores ($F = 1$).

TABLE 5
RELATION BETWEEN IMPULSIVENESS AND COLLEGE GRADES

Subject	Nonimpulsive		Moderate		Impulsive	
	$\overline{X}$	N	$\overline{X}$	N	$\overline{X}$	N
High ability	2.63	112	2.32	104	2.23	103
Low ability	1.81	101	1.89	85	1.70	119

A more exhaustive analysis of these findings, covering two years of the Delaware students' academic careers, will be given in Chapter 8, which is concerned with impulsiveness and vocational choices. Comments here are limited to the observation that as in the military settings, intelligent, but impulsive students, clearly underachieved, in comparison with equally bright nonimpulsive students. This relationship is further illustrated by the finding that among high-ability students, 33% of the nonimpulsive students, 14% of the moderates, and 11% of the impulsive students had maintained better than a B average.

Findings similar to the above were found in a second university setting

(Temple University). Students in this second study were second-term freshmen tested with both the Impulsiveness Scale and the Socialization Scale
during the first week of an introductory psychology course. Scores from the
two scales were combined into an impulsiveness index, as defined in Chapter
2. Table 6 gives the final semester grades for these students classified by
level of impulsiveness and SAT level. Classification on the SAT used a
median split of 989 or more vs. 988 or less.

An unweighted means analysis of variance of these data yielded a significant effect for ability ($p < .001$), a significant effect for impulsiveness

TABLE 6

IMPULSIVENESS AND COLLEGE GRADES AT TEMPLE UNIVERSITY

SAT score	Nonimpulsive		Moderate		Impulsive	
	$\overline{X}$	N	$\overline{X}$	N	$\overline{X}$	N
High ability	2.30	35	2.13	30	1.85	39
Low ability	1.87	42	1.78	34	1.81	39

($p < .05$), and a marginally significant interaction between these two
variables ($p < .10$).

As in prior studies, further analyses found that impulsiveness was significantly predictive of grades among high-ability students ($p < .01$), but was
not predictive among low-ability students ($p < .50$).

In a third study using 142 Temple freshmen who were also tested with
both impulsiveness measures, similar results were obtained. Among freshmen with above median SAT scores (1028+), 0% of those classified as
nonimpulsive, 60% of those classified as moderate, and 45% of those
classified as impulsive were either academic dropouts or on academic
probation by the end of the semester. Among freshmen with below median
SAT scores, the corresponding proportions dropped or on probation were
63% of the nonimpulsive students, 79% of the moderates and 50% of the
impulsive students.

Impulsiveness and Achievement: Conclusions

What conclusions can be drawn from the foregoing analyses of the
influence of impulsiveness upon achievement?

Although the magnitude of the predictions was not high, the findings were
consistent in revealing that students classified as impulsive by test score

were most likely to underachieve in a variety of training settings. Furthermore, this underachievement could not be attributed to lack of ability, since it was precisely among the more intelligent segments that impulsiveness was most clearly associated with failure.

A search of the literature has found that the moderating effects of intellectual ability are not unique to the present research. Several investigators have reported equivalent findings in such socially defined achievement areas as graduation from high school (Roessel, 1954) and college achievement (Gough, 1965; Heilbrun, 1965). As an example, Roessel reported that among more intelligent high school students, those with high *Pd* scores on the Minnesota Multi-Phasic Inventory were more likely to drop out of school than those with low *Pd* scores. Among less intelligent high school students, there was no relation between scores on the *Pd* scale and graduation from high school. Whereas Roessel based his observations upon the *Pd* scale, Gough used the Socialization and Responsibility Scales from the California Psychological Inventory; Heilbrun used the Adjective Check List to measure what he called conformity to social values. The various personality scales used in these studies appear to have in common the goal of measuring aspects of character development. Thus, it is interesting, and also reassuring, to find that different measures of what appears to be the same basic personality construct yielded equivalent findings.

Outside of the area of school achievement, there are also occasional reports that intellectual ability moderates the relation between impulsiveness and behavior. Panton (1960) for instance, examined the personality profiles of a prison population with the MMPI, using prisoners at several levels of intelligence. The MMPI profiles of the more intelligent prisoners (IQ's of 110 or more) were dominated by a configuration generally classified under the rubric of character disorders. The patterning of the MMPI scores of the average and below average IQ groups were dominated by configurations usually associated with neuroticism and anxiety.

An interesting experimental study of interpersonal dominance by Carment, Miles, and Cervin (1965) also revealed similar moderating effects for intelligence. In this study, the introversion–extroversion scale from the Maudsley Inventory was used to select subjects. Subjects were also classified by level of intelligence. Pairs of introverts and extroverts were required to come to a common agreement on an issue in which prior disagreement had been established. The findings clearly revealed that extroverts spoke more, and were less influenced by the other member of the dyad, than were introverts. However, this finding only held among more intelligent subjects. Among less intelligent subjects, introversion–extroversion was not related to interpersonal dominance.

Several possible explanations for the moderating influence of intelligence suggest themselves. In the remainder of this chapter these possibilities will be reviewed.

DIFFERENTIAL TEST VALIDITY

The first possible reason why impulsiveness does not predict among less intelligent persons is that they do not understand the various questions contained in the tests used to measure this construct. From this point of view, the reduced validity of the tests among less intelligent persons could be attributed to the fact that more errors are made by this group when answering questions. As a result, these persons are improperly classified. If this explanation is correct, however, one could expect the internal reliability of impulsiveness tests to be lower among less intelligent respondents than among more intelligent respondents. This possibility was examined by computing the split-half reliability of the Impulsiveness Scale among a sample of college students, subdivided into levels of intellectual ability. The reliability of the scale was the same at all levels of ability, suggesting no support for the above explanation.

TASK DIFFICULTY

One function of intelligence is to define how difficult a given cognitive task will be for the person. A very bright individual will generally find it easier to master his schoolwork than will the less bright individual doing the same schoolwork. As was previously pointed out in Chapter 1, there is some evidence that characterologically disturbed persons become easily distracted and rapidly bored with many tasks. Thus, it is possible that more intelligent impulsive individuals find that they can easily master their schoolwork, and hence become bored and less attentive. Contrarily, the less intelligent impulsive individual is continually presented with new challenges from his work because of its increased difficulty for him. This constant stimulation serves to hold his attention.

A laboratory experiment by Kipnis and Wagner (1965a) attempted to test this possibility by having impulsive and nonimpulsive sailors work on a series of cognitive and perceptual-motor tasks, each of which varied in task difficulty. The sailors were also grouped by level of intelligence. The findings revealed that the performance of impulsive sailors, at all levels of intelligence, was not influenced by the experimental variations in task difficulty. In short, no support was found for the task-difficulty explanation.

DEVELOPMENTAL HISTORY

It is generally accepted that a basic function of intelligence is to aid the individual in adapting to his environment. Survival favors the brighter individuals by virtue of their possession of a greater repertoire of responses that they may invoke when required to cope with problems.

In line with this view it is possible that as preadolescents, *less* intelligent boys with impulsive personality structures were more frequently detected and punished for attempting various antisocial acts. Contrarily, *more* intelligent impulsive boys were less frequently "caught in the act," because their superior planning and foresight anticipated possible flaws in their acts. Some support for this conjecture is found in McCord, McCord, and Zola's (1959) follow-up study of delinquents which reported that judges were less likely to sentence a bright boy than an average or dull boy, to a penal institution. If this explanation is correct, it would imply that the less intelligent impulsive child was reared under a regime of frequent punishments associated with his attempts to transgress. These frequent punishments perhaps served at a later age to inhibit the expression of poorly socialized forms of behavior. Not experiencing such frequent negative reinforcement as a child, the more intelligent impulsive person may be less concerned with the possibility of being punished and hence may be less inhibited. Although no data have been collected to test this view, one prediction that could be made is that less intelligent impulsive persons should report that they were punished more frequently for bad behavior than would be reported by their more intelligent counterparts.

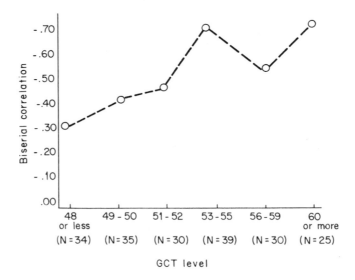

FIG. 1. Biserial correlation of Impulsiveness Scale with High School Graduation, by level of intelligence.

CHAPTER 4

Correlates of Impulsiveness

Why do bright impulsive students fail? Clearly, lack of ability is not the reason. In Chapter 3, suggestive evidence was presented that as intellectual ability increased, so too did the failure rate among impulsive persons. Furthermore, underachievement and failure cannot be attributed to a conscious desire to fail. In many conversations with bright impulsive college students, it was clear that they were disappointed by their own lack of achievement. It would appear that in order to understand this behavior one must consider the behaviors and attitudes that define the construct of impulsiveness.

As stated in Chapter 1, the literature on character-disordered personalities suggests that there are several areas of behavior and feeling that aid in the definition of this dimension. These areas are (a) the acceptance of regulatory social values, (b) restlessness and sensation-seeking behavior; (c) reactions to negative-affective stimuli; and (d) interpersonal influence processes. Fundamentally, these areas are concerned with the process of self-control and inhibition of behavior. The relation between the first three areas and impulsiveness, as measured by test scores, are presented in this chapter. Chapters 5 through 7 detail how these inhibitory processes are manifested in interpersonal relationships.

Acceptance of Conventional Values

The process of character development and growing self-awareness is closely related to the extent of the individual's identification with cultural values and goals. Furthermore, this identification with cultural values serves to guide the individual when he is tempted to carry out behaviors prohibited by these values. A common assumption is that persons fixated at earlier stages of character development are unaware of or reject common parental and cultural values. The System II individual described by Harvey, Hunt, and Schroder (1961) for instance, is considered to be oriented away from conventional social forces. Individuals at the second and third levels of ego development as described by Loevinger (1966) are also seen to be either unaware of regulatory values or to perceive them as externalized coercive forces. At successively higher stages, individuals are seen as first oriented around complete acceptance of conventional values and finally oriented around values that transcend the immediate demands of society and are based upon the identification with wider, longer-ranged, and frequently diversified human values (Lynd, 1958).

This section is concerned with identifying the kinds of conventional cultural values that are accepted or rejected by impulsive persons and non-impulsive persons. It was expected that impulsive persons would show less evidence than nonimpulsive persons of having accepted values relating to the self-regulation of behavior.

As a test of this expectation a 20-item inventory of belief in conventional middle class values and goals was administered to a sample of 333 university students. Respondents were asked to indicate how important it was for them to carry out the behavior described in each item. Answers were on a five-point scale ranging from "Of great importance" to "Of no importance." A score of one point was given to each item answered "Of great importance" or "Pretty important," with the exception of two items concerned with the acquisition of material things. A reverse scoring key was used for these two items since a preliminary tryout with sailors found that impulsive sailors rated these two items of greater importance than nonimpulsive sailors. The unit weights were summed over all 20 items to obtain a social value score for each respondent. The items were based upon statements developed by Clark and Wenninger (1963) as part of a study of values held by individuals of various social classes.

On the basis of scores on the Impulsiveness Scale, respondents were classified as impulsive (N=127); moderate (N=103); and nonimpulsive (N=103). Respondents were further subdivided into three equal levels of intellectual ability on the basis of their combined SAT scores (941 or less; 942–1063; 1064 or more). There were from 32 to 44 subjects in each of the nine cells resulting from the joint classification of respondents.

Table 7 illustrates the average social value scores of respondents. An unweighted means analysis of variance of these data yielded a significant interaction between impulsiveness and ability ($F = 2.57$, df 4/324, $p < .05$). This interaction resulted from two factors. The first was that among the most intelligent stratum of respondents, impulsive students had significantly lower social value scores than moderate or nonimpulsive students. The second factor accounting for the interaction was the rise in social value scores among impulsive students within the lowest stratum of intellectual ability. Impulsive students in this condition showed significantly greater acceptance of conventional values than impulsive students in the next two strata of intellectual ability ($p < .01$). This last finding appears consistent with the conjecture offered on page 28 that less intelligent impulsive individuals may differ from their more intelligent counterparts in that they have learned at some earlier age to accept social values which at least partially serve to inhibit impulsive behavior.

TABLE 7

AVERAGE SOCIAL VALUE SCORES BY SAT LEVEL

	Intellectual ability		
	High	Middle	Low
Behavior	$\overline{X}$	$\overline{X}$	$\overline{X}$
Impulsive	15.80	15.88	17.64
Moderate	17.25	16.85	17.73
Nonimpulsive	17.29	17.21	17.28

For respondents with SAT scores of 1064 or more, analysis of individual social value items revealed that nonimpulsive students rated as more important than impulsive students items concerned with the acceptance of internally or externally imposed standards of behavior. These items were: "to obey the rules at school or work ($p < .05$)," "to always do the things you believe are right ($p < .05$)," "to do the best you can on work assigned to you ($p < .10$)," "to have good manners and be polite ($p < .05$)," and "to be loyal to your friends ($p < .05$)."

Impulsive students rated as more important than nonimpulsive students items concerned with the acquisition of material possessions. These items were "to have modern and up-to-date things ($p < .01$)" and "to have the latest things ($p < .10$)." These latter findings are consistent with the literature cited in Chapter 1, which indicated that character-disordered personalities overvalue money and material possessions.

The greater value ascribed by impulsive individuals to material possessions was also revealed in a second study carried out among a group of
incoming university freshmen, all with SAT scores of 1000 or more. This
study will be reported in greater detail in Chapter 9. However, relevant to
the present discussion are students' responses to a set of questions asking
them how much money they estimated they would have available for weekly
living expenses during the coming semester, and how satisfied they were
with this amount. Both impulsive and nonimpulsive students, as measured
by the Impulsiveness Index, stated they would have an average of $13.00
per week available to them. However, 55% of the impulsive students and
21% of the nonimpulsive students stated they were dissatisfied with this
amount and needed more money to live on ($X^2 = 11.28$, df 1, $p < .01$). When
dissatisfied students were asked how much more money they needed,
impulsive students needed approximately one-third more money than nonimpulsive students to satisfy them. At the end of the semester these students
rated their satisfaction with the amount of money they had available during
the semester for weekly expenses. Impulsive students were once again significantly less satisfied than nonimpulsive students ($F = 9.75$, df 1/112,
$p < .01$). In short, impulsive persons appear preoccupied with money, and
more money is needed to satisfy them than is true of nonimpulsive persons.

A Behavioral Test of Norm Violation

The previous findings were based upon subjective estimates of beliefs. A
behavioral measure of how rules regulate the behavior of impulsive and
nonimpulsive students was obtained from a study of violation of university
rules concerned with class "cutting."

During the 12th week of a 16-week semester at Temple University,
attendance was taken in 21 class sections of an introductory psychology
course. All male students in these sections had taken the two measures of
impulsiveness at the beginning of the semester and the Impulsiveness Index
was used as a measure for classification of students.

In addition to examining how obeying the rules concerning absenteeism
varied as a function of impulsiveness, we were also interested in how
environmental restraints influenced conformity to these rules. Environmental restraints in this instance was defined as whether or not the instructor
habitually took attendance during the semester. It was expected that
impulsive students would conform to rules regulating attendance when
instructors took attendance, but would not conform when attendance was
not taken. This is because in the latter situation there were no penalties
attached to cutting class since the instructor had no official records. Hence,

the decision to cut class should be regulated by how seriously the individual accepted university rules concerned with attendance.

Seven instructors habitually took attendance during the semester. These instructors had 212 students in 11 class sections. The remaining five instructors had never taken attendance in their classes prior to the criterion day. These instructors had 247 students in ten class sections. It should be noted that three of the five instructors who did not take attendance, usually did so during other semesters, but refrained this semester at my request. In all, 12 instructors took attendance among 459 students; 21% of the students were absent on the day attendance was taken.

Classroom attendance was analyzed by means of a $3 \times 2 \times 2$ analysis of variance, with three levels of impulsiveness, two levels of restraint (instructors did or did not take attendance) and two levels of intellectual ability (above and below median SAT scores). Any person absent on the day attendance was taken was assigned a score of 1, and those present, a score of 0. These scores were used as the dependent measure in the analysis of variance. Table 8 presents the findings.

TABLE 8

PERCENTAGE OF STUDENTS ABSENT

SAT level	Restraint	Impulsive (%)	Moderate (%)	Non-impulsive (%)
Above median	Attendance taken	28	12	9
	Attendance not taken	37	22	19
Below median	Attendance taken	20	8	7
	Attendance not taken	33	32	22

Whether or not instructors took attendance yielded the strongest relation with absentee rate. When the instructors exercised their restraining powers by taking attendance, an average of 13% of the students were absent as compared to 27% when these powers were not used ($p < .01$). As predicted, an average of 29% of the impulsive students, 18% of the moderate students and 14% of the nonimpulsive students were absent ($p < .01$). While it had been predicted that the use of external restraints by a teacher would mainly influence the absentee rate of impulsive students, it can be observed in Table 8 that this environmental factor influenced all students equally. This latter finding can be interpreted as an indication that if the environment is perceived to contain punitive restraints against nonconformity, acts of conformity will decrease. This interpretation is consistent with more general studies of coercive power (French, Morrison, and Levinger, 1960; French and Raven, 1959; Zipf, 1965) in which it has been found that reliance by authority figures upon threats of punishment induced higher rates of public conformity than when no threats were relied upon. In essence, the taking of attendance by instructors represents an exercise of threatening power, since university regulations require punishment for excessive numbers of unexcused absences. And to the extent that attendance is taken, the probabilities are higher that students who are continually absent will be reported to the administration.

Restlessness, Sensation Seeking, Self-Control

As discussed in Chapter 1, the psychopath appears unable to tolerate routine and boredom and he requires new and exciting things to do as a means of dissipating these feelings of boredom. Quay (1965) has proposed that psychopathic behavior represents an extreme case of stimulation seeking. That is, he has hypothesized that the psychopath is in a chronic state of cortical underarousal and thereby attempts to increase arousal to some more optimal level by seeking exciting stimulations. Eysenck (1967) and Hare (1968) have offered similar explanations of the psychopath's restlessness and sensation-seeking behaviors.

One consequence of this rapid adaptation to sensory stimuli is suggested by general studies concerned with experiencing the passage of time. These studies show that when all persons become bored, time is experienced as moving slowly (Geiwitz, 1964), and that when persons are emotionally aroused, time is experienced as moving rapidly (Filer and Meals, 1949; Harton, 1939). Since psychopaths should, on the average, experience greater boredom than normals, one could expect the former group to experience unfilled time as moving more slowly than for the latter. This expectation has been supported in several studies which have required both institutionalized character-disordered individuals and normals to estimate the passage of unfilled time (Orme, 1962; Siegman, 1961). In all instances, the institutionalized groups overestimated the passage of unoccupied time. These findings then lead to the prediction that impulsive individuals should also overestimate the duration of unfilled time.

The procedure to test this hypothesis consisted of having 48 sailors sit quietly by themselves in a lighted, but small and completely soundproofed room that had been developed for sensory deprivation research. They were presented with an initial signal through earphones and were told to press a button in front of them when they estimated that 8 minutes had passed. Subjects were asked not to count as a means of estimating time.

Subjects were jointly classified on the basis of the Impulsiveness Scale and a median GCT split (53 versus 52). The dependent measure was the number of seconds that elapsed between the initial signal and sailors pressing the button to signify that 8 minutes passed. Table 9 displays these results.

TABLE 9

AVERAGE ELAPSED TIME BEFORE SIGNALING THAT 8 MINUTES HAD PASSED[a]

Intellectual ability	Impulsive	Moderate	Non-impulsive
Above median	345.00	491.10	463.60
Below median	348.50	434.50	393.00

[a] Measured in seconds.

An analysis of variance of the data in Table 9 yielded a significant effect only for level of impulsiveness ($F = 4.78$, df 2/42, $p < .05$). Nonimpulsive and moderate sailors waited for a longer period of time than did impulsive sailors before signaling that 8 minutes had passed. It may also be observed that the difference between impulsive and nonimpulsive sailors was most marked among those who were above average in intellectual ability. Separate F tests of the relation between time estimates and level of impulsiveness within each level of ability revealed that impulsiveness was significantly related to time estimates among the more intelligent ($p < .05$), but not among the less intelligent ($p < .30$).

In a second study, an attempt was made to replicate the above findings using a different setting—one in which the sensory deprivation features of the room were eliminated. Twenty impulsive, 17 moderate, and 14 non-impulsive sailors with GCT scores of 54 or better estimated the passage of 8 minutes by the method of production, while seated alone in a room in a navy barracks. Noise from the rest of the barracks was at a moderate level.

Nonimpulsive sailors waited an average of 525 seconds, moderates an average of 386 seconds, and impulsive sailors waited an average of 432 seconds before signaling that 8 minutes had passed. The analysis of variance approached significance ($p < .10$), with the major difference falling between moderately impulsive and nonimpulsive sailors ($p < .05$). Since the major difference between the two studies was the sensory deprivation setting used in the first study, it is possible that the factor of reduced sensory input enhanced the results of the first study. In general, all sailors were more variable in their estimates of time in the second study. A comparison of the variances of time estimation for the two studies yielded a significant F ratio of 2.46 (df 48/51, $p < .01$).

A final finding on the relation between stimulation seeking and impulsiveness was that in a sample of 161 sailors, the Impulsiveness Scale correlated .52 with the Sensation-Seeking Scale, developed by Zuckerman and co-workers (1964; 1968). Zuckerman has reported that persons scoring high on his scale are restless and require more stimulation from the environment to maintain an optimal level of psychological comfort. This correlational finding is of interest since the items in the two scales show little overlap, and Zuckerman has presented extensive evidence on the construct validity of his scale as a measure of the need for stimulus variability.

Affective Arousal

A frequently noted feature of persons with severe character disorders is their lack of affective response in shameful or anxiety-provoking situations. It appeared to Cleckley, for instance, that sociopaths, as a group, functioned within a rather severely restricted range of emotional arousal, and that this attentuation of affect was the cause of their inability to profit from past experience. Clerkley's convictions are also consistent with learning theorists' views of the role of anxiety reduction in mediating avoidance learning (Mowrer, 1939; Miller, 1948). At its most general level, this view states that people learn to avoid activities that will potentially produce severe feelings of anxiety, shame, guilt, and embarrassment. Of course, these situations generally involve socially prohibited activities. Since the psychopath only minimally experiences negative-affective states, his behavior is correspondingly less likely to be inhibited by these restraining forces. A summary of the experimental literature by Hare (1968) also supports the view that the psychopath shows little overt anxiety, has low levels of autonomic tension, and does not learn to avoid stressful stimuli.

In this section the findings on emotional reactivity are extended to the population at large, in terms of investigations into the relation between impulsiveness itself and several questionnaire and behavioral measures of negative-affective arousal.

Questionnaire Relationships

Three purported measures of affective arousal were related to the Impulsiveness Scale. These three measures were as follows:

THE ACTIVITY PREFERENCE INVENTORY

This is a 33-item forced-choice scale developed by Lykken (1957) for his study of the criminal psychopath. Each pair of items described two unpleasant events. One of the events is disagreeable because it is embarrassing or shameful, and the other event is also unpleasant because it arouses discomfort of a nonembarrassing nature. A typical pair of items is (a) cleaning up a spilled bottle of syrup, and (b) knocking over a glass of water in a crowded restaurant. The respondent is asked which of these two alternatives he would prefer to do. A high score indicates a consistent choice of the potentially embarrassing alternative.

THE FEAR QUESTIONNAIRE

This is a 15-item questionnaire based upon a longer form developed by Lazovik and Lang (1960).* The Questionnaire asks respondents how much they are bothered by the following things or experiences: sudden noises, angry people, high places, bats, failure, dentists, members of the opposite sex, harmless snakes, looking foolish, witnessing surgical operations, dogs, tough-looking people, fire, speaking in public, and feeling anger. Each item is answered on a four-point scale, ranging from "not at all disturbed" to "very much disturbed" (weighted 4). The questionnaire was scored by summing item scores. High scores indicated a high degree of fear arousal.

THE TAYLOR MANIFEST ANXIETY SCALE

Results

The Activity Preference Inventory was administered to 259 sailors, and the Fear Questionnaire was administered to a sample of 168 male Temple University students. Navy subjects were classified in terms of intellectual ability using GCT scores (50 or less; 51–56; 57 or more) and university students on the basis of SAT scores (941 or less; 942–1063; 1064 or more). For both samples the Impulsiveness Scale was used to classify subjects.

Table 10 shows the average Activity Preference scores and the Average Fear Questionnaire scores for subjects classified in terms of impulsiveness and intellectual ability. Analyses of variance of these two sets of scores yielded significant F ratios for the factor of impulsiveness in both instances. The F ratio for the Activity Preference scores was 9.77 (df 2/250, $p < .01$) and for the Fear Questionnaire it was 3.47 (df 2/159, $p < .05$).

It can be seen that impulsive subjects more frequently preferred the embarrassing or shameful activity to the unpleasant one on the Activity Preference inventory. They also stated that they were less bothered by the various items in the Fear Questionnaire.

Intellectual ability did not moderate the relation between impulsiveness

* This version of the scale was developed by John McBrearty.

TABLE 10

AVERAGE SCORES ON THE ACTIVITY PREFERENCE INVENTORY AND THE
FEAR QUESTIONNAIRE[a]

Intellectual ability	Activity preference			Fear questionnaire		
	Impuls.	X̄ Moder.	Nonimpuls.	Impuls.	X̄ Moder.	Nonimpuls.
High	16.00	15.96	13.71	26.14	27.41	31.20
Middle	14.81	13.46	12.96	28.21	28.44	28.16
Low	14.87	13.47	11.77	26.33	26.22	30.53

[a] High scores on the Activity Preference Inventory denote a preference for anxiety provoking situations; high scores of the Fear Questionnaire denote high fear responses.

and the Activity Preference Inventory, although it can be seen that as intellectual ability rose, more persons chose the embarrassing over the unpleasant activity. For the Fear Questionnaire, however, impulsiveness had the strongest relation with this questionnaire among high-ability subjects ($p < .05$), but was not related at this significance level among middle or low-ability subjects. However, the relation between impulsiveness and fear ratings approached significance among low-ability subjects ($p < .10$), suggesting that if intellectual ability is acting as a moderator, its influence is complex with regard to fear responses.

The final measure of affective arousal was the Manifest Anxiety Scale (MA). In two samples of 63 and 168 navy enlisted men, the overall correlations between the Impulsiveness Scale and the MA scale were .12 and .10, respectively. Both of these correlations were not significantly different from zero. An analysis of variance by impulsiveness and intellectual ability also revealed no relation between the two scales.

An examination of the nature of the items of the three measures of affective arousal suggests one possible explanation for the findings. The Activity Preference Scale and the Fear Questionnaire are concerned with the question of *frequency* of arousal. Both scales describe situations or objects that are potentially anxiety provoking and then question respondents as to how likely these situations are to bother them. The MA scale, on the other hand, is concerned with the question of *intensity* of arousal. This scale is composed of items describing anxiety symptoms and asks respondents how many of these symptoms they have experienced. The findings suggest that although impulsive and nonimpulsive persons may experience equally intense anxiety reactions, there are fewer objects and situations capable of eliciting such anxiety responses in impulsive than in nonimpulsive persons. That is, fewer things bother the impulsive person.

Public Speaking

In the next study we investigated a situation that has high potential for eliciting fear reactions and determined the differential influence of this situation upon impulsive and nonimpulsive participants. The situation was speaking in classrooms. It may be recalled that in response to the Fear Questionnaire, impulsive persons said that one of the situations that would not annoy them was speaking in public. One test of this assertion is to obtain teachers' observations of who is most visible in their classrooms, by virtue of their constant speaking. Presumably, impulsive students would be the talkers.

To this end, nine instructors teaching 13 sections of introductory psychology were asked to rate all male students in terms of classroom participation. There were between 20 and 28 male students in each section; the evaluations were made in the ninth and tenth weeks of the school term. Students had been previously tested using both the Impulsiveness Scale and the Socialization Scale and scores from both scales were combined into the Impulsiveness Index.

The instructors were asked to circle the names of all students in their classes who matched the descriptions given on the rating forms. The descriptions read as follows:

FACILITATIVE BEHAVIOR

"Some students contribute to the teaching process by asking reasonable questions or by making constructive comments. Circle the names of students who fit this description."

DISRUPTIVE BEHAVIORS

"Some students disrupt classroom proceedings by asking inappropriate or hostile questions, by obvious inattention, or by other kinds of disruptive acts. Circle the names of students who fit this description."

In addition to impulsiveness and intellectual ability, the ratings were analyzed in terms of whether students were freshmen or upper classmen. The classification of students in terms of class level was added to test the generally held belief that freshmen participate less in classroom discussions than do upper classmen.

For each student a score of 1 was given if the instructor checked his name on a given scale, and a score of 0, if his name was not checked. This score was used as the dependent measure in a $3 \times 2 \times 2$ analysis of variance, with impulsiveness as the first factor, freshmen versus upperclassmen as the second, and intellectual ability as the third factor. Overall, the number of students evaluated as contributing to classroom discussions (14%) or evaluated as disruptive (9%) was remarkably low. Two percent of the students were seen as both contributing to classroom discussion and as being disruptive. To instructors then, the vast majority of students in their classes were invisible.

Table 11 shows the findings in terms of the percentages of students nominated by instructors as contributing to classroom proceedings. As can be seen, facilitative behavior was mainly limited to high-ability upperclassmen. Furthermore, within the high-ability upperclass group, 53% of the impulsive students, 19% of the moderates, and 22% of the nonimpulsive students were rated as contributing to the classroom discussions ($p < .05$ by F test). This latter finding is consistent with the prediction that impulsive students would speak more in class. However, it appears that in terms of constructive behaviors, the prediction holds only among more intelligent upperclassmen.

TABLE 11

PERCENTAGE OF STUDENTS EVALUATED AS CONTRIBUTING TO
CLASS DISCUSSIONS

Class level	Intellectual ability	Impulsive (%)	Moderate (%)	Nonimpulsive (%)	Average (%)
Freshmen	Above median	8	6	16	10
	Below median	3	15	8	9
Upperclass-men	Above median	53	19	22	30
	Below median	16	5	17	13

The second rating asked instructors to nominate those students in their classes whose behavior was disruptive of classroom proceedings. Table 12 summarizes these ratings. The analysis of variance yielded a significant interaction between class level and impulsiveness ($p < .05$). Among freshmen, impulsive students were nominated more frequently than moderate or nonimpulsive students as being disruptive. Among upperclassmen, there was no consistent relation between impulsive and disruptive behavior. These findings are again consistent with the prediction that impulsive students would be more visible to their instructors than nonimpulsive students. However, in terms of disruptive behavior, the findings indicate that this prediction only holds among freshmen.

TABLE 12

PERCENTAGE OF STUDENTS NOMINATED AS DISRUPTIVE BY THE INSTRUCTORS

Class level	Intellectual ability	Impulsive (%)	Moderate (%)	Nonimpulsive (%)
Freshmen	Above median	21	6	0
	Below median	17	4	5
Upperclassmen	Above median	6	21	6
	Below median	8	5	0

To summarize, the findings support the notion that impulsive students would be more visible in class than nonimpulsive students because they were more verbal. We assume that lowered feelings of anxiety facilitated this greater verbal output. Unexpectedly, however, the findings revealed that the content of this verbal output varied as a function of the student's intelligence and class level. As freshmen, instructors considered the verbal output of impulsive students to be disruptive. Presumably their comments were hostile or designed to "get laughs" from fellow students, or were inappropriate to the lecture, and the like. As upperclassmen, instructors appeared to welcome the comments from bright impulsive students. Something had changed—some form of social learning appears to have occurred among impulsive students. Perhaps they learned to modify their verbal output so that what they said was more acceptable to their instructors. Another obvious possibility, of course, is that those impulsive students who were considered as disruptive in their freshmen year were dropped from the university and different impulsive students were considered facilitative in subsequent years. Unfortunately, we do not have data on the classroom behavior of the same students over a period of several years. Such information would be necessary to clarify the basis for the shift in evaluations.

Summary

In this chapter we have examined various sources that act to restrain impulsive behavior. These sources consisted of restraints that originate in the acceptance of social norms and values, restraints that originate from differences in the amount of excitement and stimulation needed to maintain psychological comfort, and restraints that originate in the desire of individuals to avoid experiencing negative-affective states such as anxiety or embarrassment. Impulsive individuals were less influenced by these various sources of restraint than were nonimpulsive individuals.

Evidence was also presented suggesting that impulsive individuals could exercise control over their behavior if the situation demanded it. This conclusion is based upon the study in which situational restraints were imposed upon behavior in the form of attendance taking by teachers. This source of restraint produced improved attendance. If we view the inhibition of behavior as a joint function of personal controls and environmental restraints, we might then expect impulsive individuals to show control when environmental restraints are present, but not when personal controls are involved.

We initially raised the question as to why bright impulsive students failed. The cluster of behaviors investigated in this chapter are clearly antagonistic to the classical day-to-day diligence required of college students. Haphazard classroom attendance and sporadic study habits because of boredom are obvious causes of underachievement. On the positive side, however, the findings revealed that in terms of classroom participation, it was the impulsive students whose comments and remarks as upperclassmen) were appreciated by instructors. If anything, nonimpulsive students appeared overrestrained and inhibited in these situations. Their behavior reminds me of the many silent and almost invisible students in some of my classes who first call attention to themselves by achieving the highest grades on tests and quizzes. Yet it is almost impossible to induce these students to participate in classroom discussions. When persuaded to talk, their remarks are brief and are not designed to encourage prolonged exchanges. Whereas the reader may note then that up to this point we have been speaking in primarily negative terms about impulsive individuals as underachievers, poorly controlled, and the like, we can see here that the issue is not that simple. The same behaviors that perhaps contribute to their underachievement in grades may facilitate their achievement in nonacademic matters.

CHAPTER 5

Interpersonal Sources of Influence

Chapter 4 dealt mainly with various intrapersonal sources of restraint as these influenced the behavior of impulsive and nonimpulsive persons. The next three chapters are concerned with how the behavior of impulsive persons are restrained or influenced by other persons.

Basically, our assumptions about the influence of others are drawn from several sources. Over the last 20 years or so a large body of research concerned with small group processes has been reported. These studies reveal the very real influence exerted by face-to-face relationships upon individual cognitions, attitudes, and feelings. Furthermore, these studies have provided a fair understanding of situational conditions that facilitate interpersonal influence processes. Unfortunately, these studies have provided less information on individual differences in this regard. There are several reasons for this. First of all, small group research has drawn its theoretical orientation primarily from homestatic theory in physiology, with its focus upon general regulatory processes. In its classical form this theory has not addressed itself to the problems of individual differences. A second and more pragmatic reason for this lack of attention has been that individual difference measures have not accounted for too much of the variance in group studies. Among the reasons for this state of affairs, I believe, is the fact that the design of small group experiments has tended to contrast massively different situational effects (e.g., cohesive versus noncohesive groups) which dominate the individual's response and tend to evoke the same response from all persons in that condition. It appears to me that individual differences become important when the strength of the evoking situational stimuli is around the average response threshhold of the group under study. Under these circumstances, variations in threshhold sensitivity to the evoking situational stimuli are likely to determine who will respond. As an example, one could predict that a measure of trait anxiety would be more important as a determinant of panic behavior in a theater when there were but 25 patrons and 20 exits at the time a small fire was discovered, than when there were 500 patrons and ten exits in the theater. The former situation should evoke anxiety and panic responses from only the most anxiety-prone persons, whereas the latter situation should evoke these emotions from all. Thus, personality becomes important as the situation becomes less compelling.

In any case, the social psychological literature has not been particularly revealing about the effects of individual differences upon group influence processes. However, the clinical literature, and to a lesser extent the experimental literature, cited in Chapter 1, does indicate that character-disordered persons are less open than normals to advice, suggestions, and direction from others. Taking our cue from this evidence we predict that compared with nonimpulsive persons, impulsive persons would not be as likely to accept influence from others—especially if this influence was intended to restrain their behavior.

The Influence of Friends and Peers

FIRST STUDY

Adolescence is a time in which many individuals are influenced by peers and are prone to question parental advice. Part of the reported success of peer influence, however, may occur because the adolescents are already tempted to carry out the behaviors advocated by peers, but are still restrained by parental or social prohibitions. Hence, the peers' instigations are consistent with the adolescent's own inclinations. As such, the notorious influence of peers in directing persons away from parental values may be overrated.

Our first study along these lines was an attempt to investigate how peers might influence the judgment of impulsive and nonimpulsive subjects, when these judgments were at odds. Under these conditions, an agreement reached between subjects and peers truly represents the influence of one person upon the other, rather than the persuasion of one person toward a direction to which he was already attracted. It was expected that the impulsive subject would be less influenced by peers or friends than would nonimpulsive subjects for reasons presented above.

The first phase of the study involved asking groups of 15 impulsive and 15 nonimpulsive male university students, with SAT scores of 1000 or more, to bring a close male friend to the laboratory. Impulsiveness was measured by the Impulsiveness Index. Subjects and friends were told that the purpose of the study was to investigate team influence upon the perception of light movement. At the laboratory each dyad judged both individually and as a team the movement of light based upon the autokinetic effect.

Before making these judgments however, an attempt was made to assess the extent of friendship that existed between the subject and his friend. Each subject was asked how long he had been a friend of the person with him today. A second question asked all respondents to rate the closeness of their friendship, using the following scale: my best friend; one of my good friends; a friend; an acquaintance; though we like each other, we don't know each other too well. The ratings of friendship were scored by assigning weights of 1 to 5 to each response alternative (my best friend=5). There were no significant differences between impulsive and nonimpulsive subjects on these two measures of friendship.

An index of friendship was developed by assigning a score of one point for each 12 months of friendship (range 1 to 5) and combining this score with the ratings of closeness of friendship. Friendships that had lasted beyond 60 months were given a score of 5.

Interpersonal influence was measured in terms of the extent to which subjects and their friends converged in their judgments of the distance that the pinpoint of light appeared to move. Subjects and their friends were first trained individually as a means of establishing differing standards of judgments. During this individual session, each subject was trained to judge that the light had moved more than 10 inches during each 5-second trial. His friend, on the other hand, was trained to judge that the light had moved less than 3 inches during each trial. Training was accomplished by providing false feedback information after each judgment made by the person on ten training trials.

Following the individual training, members of each dyad were seated side-by-side and judged the light movement as a team for ten trials of 5-second duration. On the first trial the subject called out his estimate first, followed by the friend. On the second trial the friend called out his estimate first, followed by the subject. This alternation of subject and friend continued for ten trials.

RESULTS

We first compared the extent to which impulsive and nonimpulsive subjects conformed to their friends' judgments. Conformity for subjects was indicated by a decrease in estimates of the distance the light moved. The general trend of the results was for nonimpulsive subjects to converge on their friends' judgments more than impulsive subjects. Furthermore, non-impulsive subjects showed more and more convergence as the experiment progressed. A repeated-measures analysis of variance of the above data yielded a significant interaction between trials and impulsiveness ($p < .01$). By the last block of trials, nonimpulsive subjects had converged on their friends' judgments to a significantly greater extent than had impulsive subjects (see Table 13).

We also examined whether good friends or casual acquaintances had a greater influence on each other. This was done by classifying each dyad as being composed of good friends or acquaintances on the basis of a median split on the Friendship Index. It was found that the closer the friendship between nonimpulsive subjects and their friends, the more readily non-impulsive subjects changed their judgment of the light movement to coincide with that of their friends ($p < .01$). Closeness of friendship did not influence the judgments of impulsive subjects. That is, their estimates did not change any more for good friends than for acquaintances (Table 13).

How did friends react to the disparity in judgments between themselves and subjects? To answer this question, the convergence scores for friends of impulsive and nonimpulsive subjects were compared. Convergence in this instance was indicated by upward shifts in the friends' estimates of light movement.

The analysis of variance found a significant difference between the judgment of friends of impulsive and nonimpulsive subjects ($p < .05$). From the 3rd–4th block of trials to the last block (9th–10th) friends of impulsive subjects showed greater convergence on their partner's judgments than did the friends of nonimpulsive subjects.

In short, the findings revealed that impulsive subjects were less influenced by friends than were nonimpulsive subjects. Furthermore, the friends of impulsive subjects gave way in their judgments more often than the friends of nonimpulsive subjects. This would suggest that the impulsive subjects were the more dominant members of the friendship pairs.

SECOND STUDY

The independence of judgment shown by impulsive subjects could have been due to the fact that impulsive subjects selected a friend who was sub-missive, while nonimpulsive subjects selected less submissive friends. To test the generality of the findings, a second study employed male and female strangers (actually confederates of the experimenters) who attempted to influence impulsive and nonimpulsive subjects to change their estimates of the light movement on the autokinetic task. In addition, control groups of impulsive and nonimpulsive subjects gave their own judgments of the amount of light movement, after having been trained for ten trials to perceive large light movements. The control groups provided baselines against which to estimate the absolute amount of influence exerted by the confederates.

The inclusion of a female stranger in this second study was based upon the suggestive evidence mentioned in Chapter 1 that character-disordered individuals may be influenced by opportunities to interact with the opposite sex. If this is so, this influence should manifest itself in the present study by impulsive subjects altering their judgments for the female stranger, but not for the male stranger.

There were 16 impulsive and 16 nonimpulsive subjects in the study, with half of each group teamed with the male confederate and half with the female confederate. As in the previous study, subjects were first trained individually to perceive large light movements. Then the subjects and confederates made team judgments. In a matter-of-fact tone the confederate consistently reported that the light moved from 1 to 3 inches. In the control condition, seven impulsive and seven nonimpulsive subjects were trained to

TABLE 13

JUDGMENTS OF THE AUTOKINETIC EFFECT[a]

	Blocks of trials				
Team condition	1–2	3–4	5–6	7–8	9–10
	Impulsive subjects				
Good friend (N = 7)	24.86	20.57	20.86	16.86	19.71
Acquaintance (N = 8)	25.87	23.38	19.38	17.38	20.38
Male stranger (N = 8)	26.37	30.25	23.25	23.63	26.50
Female stranger (N = 8)	26.75	24.00	21.13	17.63	17.12
Control (N = 7)	26.57	26.00	25.86	22.71	27.57
	Nonimpulsive subjects				
Good friends (N = 7)	21.28	16.43	13.86	15.14	11.43
Acquaintance (N = 8)	26.87	21.88	21.88	20.25	16.87
Male stranger (N = 8)	24.75	19.38	19.38	19.25	15.38
Female stranger (N = 8)	22.00	19.75	17.13	18.13	15.63
Control (N = 7)	21.29	21.57	26.43	23.57	27.29

[a] Lower scores equal convergence on other person's judgment.

see large light movements; afterward they gave judgments for ten trials seated by themselves.

Table 13 shows the average judgments of subjects over blocks of trials. In addition, Table 13 presents the judgments of subjects from the first study. These latter subjects were divided on the basis of the Friendship Index (median split) into those who brought either a good friend or an acquaintance into the laboratory.

The analysis revealed that by the last block of trials, nonimpulsive subjects had converged on the judgments of male strangers and good friends to a significantly greater extent ($p < .01$) than had impulsive subjects. Impulsive and nonimpulsive subjects, however, did not differ significantly in the extent to which their estimates converged with acquaintances ($p < .10$) and female strangers ($p < .30$).

The next comparisons were considered in terms of the absolute amount of opinion changes that occurred, based upon comparisons with the control groups. Compared to their control group, impulsive subjects were significantly influenced by the presence of good friends ($p < .05$), acquaintances ($p < .05$), and female strangers ($p < .01$). However, male strangers did not influence impulsive subjects to deviate from judgments made in their control condition. For nonimpulsive subjects, all experimental pairings influenced them to change their estimates of light movements $p < .01$).

DOMINANCE

Aside from being relatively uninfluenced by their friends, the first study revealed that impulsive subjects strongly influenced their friends' judgments. Further information on the relative dominance of impulsive and nonimpulsive subjects was gathered from a questionnaire filled out by subjects and their friends at the end of the autokinetic session. The questionnaires were completed by subjects and friends working independently of each other.

The ten items in the questionnaire were concerned with dominance behavior. Each question was answered on a 9-point scale ranging from "rarely" to "all the time." These items were concerned with such activities as "telling your friend that you strongly disagree with him," "seeing what your friend thinks before taking a stand," "making the final decision ln a disagreement," "being the one who suggests places to go," "taking the lead in activities," and similar items. The ten items were scored to give an index of dominance.* The higher the score, the greater the indication that respondents assumed the dominant role in the friendship relations.

---

* The questionnaire originally contained 13 items. An item analysis against total score revealed that three items did not correlate with this total score. These three items were discarded.

The comparison of the dominant score of impulsive and nonimpulsive subjects was made at two levels of friendship, using a median split on the Friendship Index. Among acquaintances, there was no difference between impulsive and nonimpulsive subjects in the extent to which they reported they dominated their friends. However, among good friends, as measured by the Friendship Index, impulsive subjects had an average dominance score of 57.00 as compared to 46.00 for nonimpulsive subjects. This difference was significant beyond the .05 level. Impulsive subjects then were more likely than nonimpulsive subjects to state that they exercised control over decisions made with their good friends.

Peer Influence on Aggressive Behavior

The next study of peer influence is concerned with instigation to aggression. The difference between this study and the preceding one is that in the present instance, peers were trying to influence impulsive persons to behave in a manner that they were already tempted to carry out. Of central interest in this study was the finding that peers had *more* rather than *less* influence upon the behavior of impulsive persons.

The findings were drawn from a study by Wheeler (Wheeler, 1966; Wheeler and Caggiula, 1966) designed to test conditions influencing the contagion of aggressive behavior. Wheeler has proposed that contagion occurs when an individual is first aroused to carry out some prohibited act and then observes a model carry out the act without being punished. The model's behavior and subsequent avoidance of punishment is assumed to lower the individual's own restraints against carrying out the act. Implicit in Wheeler's model is the assumption that persons who have lower inner restraints against performing socially disapproved acts will show greater contagion of behavior after observing the model, than will persons with higher inner restraints. This assumption then leads to the obvious prediction that impulsive subjects will show greater contagion of behavior than nonimpulsive subjects, under conditions stated by Wheeler.

In Wheeler and Caggiula's study, 188 sailors were placed in a communication net with two other persons, each simulated by a tape recorder. The sailors were told that they were to exchange opinions on six topics—religion, war, parents, sex, liquor, and marital roles. Sailors were also required to evaluate the stated opinions of the other two members of the communications net. These evaluations were to be done verbally so that the other members could perceive.

In essence there were two sets of conditions. In one set, which we refer to as the low-restraint condition, sailors heard the first simulated person express extremely deviant opinions, which invariably aroused the sailors to anger.

They further heard the second simulated person (the model) attack the first simulated person in an extremely hostile and aggressive manner for holding such extreme views.

In the second set of conditions, the high-restraint condition, the model either did not verbally aggress against the first simulated person, or the first simulated person's views were very mild and did not provoke anger among the sailors, although he was verbally attacked by the model.

Sailors were classified as impulsive, moderate, or nonimpulsive on the basis of the Impulsiveness Scale. Information on their level of intellectual ability was not available at the time of the analysis. The dependent measure was based upon a content analysis of each sailor's verbal evaluation of the first simulated person. An index of aggression was developed by combining all sailors' remarks that were coded as moderately aggressive (scored 2) or extremely aggressive (scored 3).

Wheeler and Caggiula expected sailors to show more contagion of aggressive behavior in the low-restraint than in the high-restraint conditions. Further prediction in the present analysis was that impulsive sailors would restrain their aggression less than would nonimpulsive sailors.

Table 14 shows the average aggression index score for sailors classified in terms of impulsiveness and conditions of restraint. As Wheeler and Caggiula reported, there was very little aggression in the high-restraint condition. The

TABLE 14

AVERAGE NUMBER OF AGGRESSIVE REMARKS DIRECTED AT THE
FIRST CONFEDERATE

Conditions	Impulsive		Moderate		Nonimpulsive	
	$\bar{X}$	N	$\bar{X}$	N	$\bar{X}$	N
Low-restraint	11.17	29	8.06	33	8.33	27
High-restraint	3.37	3 8	2.75	20	2.49	41

reanalysis of their data also revealed that in both the high- and low-restraint conditions, impulsive sailors were more easily instigated to express aggression than were moderate or nonimpulsive sailors. Analysis of variance yielded a significant F ratio for the factor of impulsiveness ($p < .05$). Separate analyses of variance within each of the experimental conditions revealed that impulsiveness related to the expression of aggression beyond the .01 level in the low-restraint condition and was not related to verbal aggression in the high-restraint condition ($F < 1$).

In short then, the results revealed that when sailors observed a model directing aggressive remarks at the source of the irritation, after having been provoked to anger, impulsive subjects were more likely than nonimpulsive subjects to imitate the model's aggressive behavior. These findings are consistent with the assumption that impulsive individuals have lower inner restraints against violating normative kinds of behavior than nonimpulsive individuals. Hence, they are more easily persuaded by peers to translate their impulses into action. As we shall see, this set of circumstances is the only instance uncovered in our research indicating that other persons had more influence over impulsive than nonimpulsive persons.

The Influence of Appointed Leaders

It seems evident from the behaviors presented in the previous section that impulsive persons will be less likely to modify their behavior merely to please their peers. In this section we will see that the same generalization holds when legitimate leaders attempt to modify their behavior.

French and Raven (1959) point out that obeying orders from legitimate authority is based upon a complex set of internalized values that produce a feeling that one "ought" to obey. If we assume that impulsive individuals are less likely to have internalized the kinds of values that produce this feeling of "oughtness," then one can predict that impulsive individuals should be less accepting of orders from legitimately appointed leaders. Of course we do not expect this prediction to hold under all circumstances. For instance, suppose that the appointed leader threatened to punish non-compliance. Under these circumstances one might predict that impulsive persons would comply as a means of avoiding the threatened punishment. Presumably the stronger the threat, the more likely the impulsive person would be to comply. In short, we would predict that influence attempts by leaders may have more success among impulsive persons when based upon coercive powers than when based upon powers derived from the legitimacy of their positions.

An experiment to test these predictions was carried out among sailors by Carl Wagner and myself. These sailors had volunteered to come to the Navy Medical Research Unit, Bethesda, Maryland, to help in the development of selection tests. After taking several tests (including the Impulsiveness Scale), the sailors were temporarily assigned to help the regular navy staff on the pretext that the civilian experimenter had to go to a meeting. The sailors were assigned work filling in mark-sense IBM cards based upon long lists of hospital supplies.

They were assigned to work for a petty officer who varied in his ability to punish noncompliance. In the first condition (nonsupport), the sailors witnessed an attempt on the part of the petty officer to deprive an enlisted man of an afternoon pass. This was accomplished by staging a scene between the enlisted man and the petty officer (both confederates) after the sailors had been working on their task for 30 minutes. The claim of the petty officer was that he could not spare the enlisted man that afternoon, but would give him time off another day. This attempt to deprive the enlisted man of his time off was invariably viewed by the subjects as an unfair punitive act.

After a few minutes of argument between the petty officer and the enlisted man, both left to have the matter settled by a senior noncommissioned officer. A short time later the enlisted man returned (ostensibly to pick up his hat) and told the waiting sailors that he had been given his pass by the senior noncommissioned officer. He also reported that the petty officer was being bawled out for his actions. In the general conversation it was brought out that the petty officer was very weak and his decisions were never backed up by higher authority. In essence, the sailors perceived that they were working for a weak leader whose influence did not have to be taken too seriously.

In a second condition (support) the sailors witnessed the same scene. However, this time the enlisted man returned and told them that he had not been given his pass. Communicated to the sailors was the fact that anything the petty officer decided to do was "backed up" by higher-ups.

In a third condition (control) the sailors did not witness the preceding scene. The subjects were merely given a rest period at the time the above interactions took place.

Following this scene the petty officer returned and ordered the men back to work. During the next half-hour of work he ordered the sailors to work faster twice because the civilian experimenter was to return shortly and he needed to complete the job. The dependent measures used in this study was the gain in error-free production from the half-hour work period prior to

TABLE 15

GAINS IN PERFORMANCE FROM THE PREEXPERIMENTAL TO
POSTEXPERIMENTAL PERIOD[a]

Leadership condition	Impulsive	Nonimpulsive
Nonsupport	6.54	9.45
Control	6.72	12.54
Support	11.09	6.09

[a] Eleven sailors per cell.

the introduction of the experimental scene to the postscene work period. There were 33 impulsive and 33 nonimpulsive subjects randomly assigned to each of the three experimental conditions.

Table 15 shows the average gain scores made by sailors. The higher the score the greater the improvement in error-free production.

It may be seen that impulsive sailors showed the greatest improvement in their performance when working for a leader who was able to reinforce his orders with threats of punishment. Nonimpulsive sailors worked best for the leader who relied only on his legitimate right to ask for compliance. Interestingly enough, when the leader attempted to use his punitive powers in what was perceived as an unfair manner, the performance of nonimpulsive persons dropped by half. We interpret these findings to mean that when the leader acted in an unfair manner, he reduced the perceived legitimacy of his authority and consequently reduced the basis for influencing nonimpulsive sailors.

Statistical analyses of these data supported the above impression. In the control condition, nonimpulsive sailors significantly outperformed impulsive sailors ($p < .05$), whereas impulsive sailors did better in the support condition ($p < .10$). Furthermore, the gain in performance among impulsive sailors was significant at the .07 level, whereas the drop in performance of nonimpulsive sailors was significant beyond the .05 level. In general, the findings were consistent with the prediction that impulsive sailors would respond to the situation in terms of the punitive power controlled by the leader, but nonimpulsive sailors would respond in terms of the legitimacy of his actions.

Error Rate

The preceding findings were based upon the analysis of error-free production. When production was analyzed in terms of total number of mark-sense cards filled out, regardless of error rate, no significant differences by personality or by leadership conditions were found. This suggests that some sailors may have overtly complied with the leader, while covertly resisting his influence by making coding errors, that could not be immediately detected. To investigate this possibility, the percentage of errors was computed for the total mark-sense cards that each sailor completed. This percent-error score was computed separately for periods 1 and 2 and for periods 3 and 4 for each sailor.

It was found that during the first two periods, 3% of the mark-sense cards produced by nonimpulsive sailors and 7% of the cards produced by impulsive sailors contained errors. Although these differences were small, an analysis of variance of percent-error scores (converted to their arc-sign equivalents) revealed that the difference in error-rate between impulsive and nonimpusive sailors was significant beyond the .05 level. There were no differences in percent-error scores between leadership conditions ($F < 1$).

Subsequent to the introduction of the experimental manipulations, impulsive sailors continued to make significantly more errors than nonimpulsive sailors in both the Control and Nonsupport conditions (average of 11% of impulsive and 3% for nonimpulsive sailors, ($p < .05$). However, in the Support condition the percent-error rate of impulsive sailors fell to 6% and the error rate of nonimpulsive sailors rose to 6%. This latter finding suggests that the improved performance of impulsive sailors in the Support condition was not a function of merely increasing their total output of mark-sense cards, while maintaining the same error rate. Rather, it was due to an improvement in the reliability of their performance.

Advice from Counselors

In this section, findings are presented on the frequency with which university students sought the help of professional student counselors at a university counseling center. The data are based upon the 628 University of Delaware freshmen whose academic performance was reported upon in Chapter 3. It may be recalled that more intelligent impulsive students had lower final grades than equally intelligent nonimpulsive students by the end of their freshmen years. Thus, one might anticipate that a greater number of these impulsive students would seek professional help for improving their grades. On the other hand, there appear to be several equally cogent reasons for which impulsive students might not seek counseling. First, it has already been reported that impulsive individuals are less bothered by psychic distress, which generally underlies motivations to seek counseling. In addition, the previous studies in this chapter would lead to the prediction that impulsive individuals would not willingly seek out situations in which others would give them advice as to what to do.

Because of professional responsibilities to their student-clients, the university student counseling center would not identify by name individuals who had been seen at the center. However, the center did agree to inspect lists of names of the 628 freshmen, jointly classified by level of impulsiveness and by SAT scores,* and indicate how many students in each group had been seen in counseling. Table 16 gives the proportion of students, classified by impulsiveness and by ability, who sought counseling during their freshmen year. It can be seen that a greater proportion of nonimpulsive than

* Identifying classifications were not given the counseling center.

impulsive students contacted the counseling center. Surprisingly, there was little difference in the proportions of high- and low-ability students who sought counseling help, despite the fact that greater proportions of less intelligent students experienced difficulties in their work.

TABLE 16

Proportions of Students Who Received Counseling[a]

Ability	Impulsive (%)	Moderate (%)	Nonimpulsive (%)
High	26	33	36
Low	26	24	39

[a] N = 628.

To test the significance of these data, a score of 1 was given to each student who received counseling and a score of 0 was given to each student not seeking counseling. The 1 or 0 scores were used as a dependent measure in a 3×2 unweighted means analysis of variance, with three levels of impulsiveness as the first factor and two levels of ability as the second. Only the F ratio for impulsiveness was statistically significant beyond the .05 level ($F=3.19$; $df=2$ and 622), supporting the hypothesis that impulsive students were less likely than nonimpulsive students to seek counseling help. Unfortunately, we do not have any breakdowns on the reasons why students were seen at the counseling center. It seems reasonable to expect that non-impulsive students would seek counseling because of subjective feelings of discomfort and anxiety more frequently than impulsive students.

The Influence of Praise and Money

The previous studies examined the ways in which various target persons might change the behavior of impulsive individuals. In the next study Simpkins (1968) examined the influence of two frequently used incentives for changing behavior. These were the use of social praise and money. Praise and various ego-related forms of rewards have traditionally been seen as a major means of instituting behavioral changes. Both in teaching (Kennedy and Wilcutt, 1964) and in industry (Vroom, 1964), the use of commendations is considered effective means of consolidating desired changes in behavior. By the same token, the use of money is also well recognized as a change agent. In his very early studies on increasing worker output, for example, Taylor (1911) demonstrated how money served to motivate employees to efforts far beyond their normal levels.

Simpkins' prediction was that money would be an effective change agent among impulsive individuals, whereas praise was less likely to be as effective. This prediction was derived from the literature cited in Chapter 1 to the effect that money has positive incentive value, and praise has aversive properties among character-disordered individuals. Other evidence for this prediction in which impulsive individuals stressed the personal value of material rewards is cited in Chapter 4.

An experimental study provided weak support for Simpkins' prediction. The subjects were 26 impulsive and 26 nonimpulsive male university students, classified on the basis of the Impulsiveness Index. All subjects had SAT scores of 1000 or more. The procedure involved use of a modified verbal conditioning task, developed by Taffel (1955). Subjects listened to instructions presented on tape by a male described as a college professor of English. By means of remotely controlled slides, subjects were shown 80 cards containing a verb and the six pronouns I, We, You, He, She, and They. Their task consisted of constructing one short simple sentence for each slide, beginning with one of the pronouns and using the verb. To ensure the same rate of use of critical pronouns, the two pronouns used by each subject with a median frequency during the initial 20 unreinforced trials, were chosen as those to be reinforced during the next 60 acquisition trials.

Social praise as a reinforcement involved prerecorded comments of "good," "that's good," "very good," "excellent," or "fine" by the college professor who was presumably listening in another room. One of these social reinforcers was used each time the subject used one of the critical pronouns in constructing a sentence. In the money reinforcement condition, subjects received 15¢ each time they used the critical pronouns—obviously a profitable exchange for the subjects, since there was a total of 60 trials in which reinforcements were used.

The dependent measure used was the change in frequency of using the critical pronouns from the first block of 20 unreinforced trials to the last block of 20 reinforced trials. Table 17 demonstrates these changes.

It can be seen that all subjects showed sharp increases in the use of the

TABLE 17

CHANGES IN THE USE OF THE REINFORCED PRONOUN[a]

Subject	Praise	Money
Impulsive	2.85	11.23
Nonimpulsive	5.85	11.15

[a] Trials 61–80 minus trials 1–20.

critical pronouns when reinforced with money. The few subjects who did not show this increment in postinterviews were just not aware of the contingencies.

Much less behavioral change was induced by the use of verbal praise. In this instance, at least, money was far more potent than praise as a means of changing behavior. The question of interest to Simpkins, however, was whether impulsive and nonimpulsive subjects responded differently to praise. It can be seen that impulsive subjects used the critical pronouns to a lesser degree than nonimpulsive subjects when praised. Although the difference between the two groups was in the predicted direction, it was only marginally significant ($p < .10$). However, a trend analysis from the first to last block of trials demonstrated that nonimpulsive subjects significantly increased their use of the pronoun when reinforced by praise ($p < .01$), whereas impulsive subjects' use of the critical pronoun did not increase significantly over this period of time ($p < .30$).

Thus, whereas the results pointed in the direction predicted by Simpkins, they were statistically weak insofar as the direct comparisons between impulsive and nonimpulsive subjects were nonsignificant. Perhaps the finding of major interest was the large influence that money exerted on behavior. Almost all subjects were agreeable to changing their behavior in the direction advocated by the experimenter in exchange for money. Modern-day psychology, I believe, does not place too much emphasis on money as a source of motivation. The economic man has been comfortably buried since the days of Elton Mayo's well-known studies at the Hawthorne Plant of Western Electric (Roethlisberger, Dickson, Wright, 1949). But Simpkins' findings tempt one to speculate that the burial may have been premature. We shall return to this finding in Chapter 9, in which we discuss a field study that used money as a means of maintaining achievement motivation among impulsive university students.

Impulsiveness and Internal–External Control

Rotter (1966) has presented evidence that persons who believe that external events (luck, fate, or chance) determines the kinds of rewards or reinforcements they receive, tend to be more impressionable than those who believe that the reinforcements received are based upon their own efforts. Rotter explains this relationship with his statement that those who believe they control their own reinforcements feel deprived of some of this control when subjected to influence from others. Hence, they resist influence in order to maintain control over their lives. Rotter's findings appear to parallel those presented in the present chapter and suggest a relationship between impulsiveness and beliefs about locus of control of reinforcements. That is, impulsive persons should score low on Rotter's Internal–External Control Scale (I–E Scale), since low scores on the Internal–External Control Scale indicate an internal orientation with respect to the perceived locus of reinforcements.

Subjects were 29 male Temple University students with SAT scores of 980 or more. They were administered the Rotter I–E Scale and the two measures of impulsiveness during a class period. The results revealed a triangular relation between the I–E Scale and the Impulsiveness Index. Nonimpulsive students all tended to have high I–E scores; moderate and impulsive students had both high and low I–E scores. As a crude measure of the relationship between the two measures, I–E scores were dichotomized at the median of the distribution (11 or more versus 10 or less), and a biserial correlation was computed between the Impulsiveness Index and this dichotomized criterion. The resultant biserial correlation was — .43 ($p < .05$), suggesting that nonimpusive persons were more likely to believe that fate controled the kinds of reinforcements they received.

Summary

From the several studies presented, it seems clear that impulsive persons are less likely to respond positively to attempts by others to change their behavior if they are not so inclined initially. Friends, teachers, and supervisors were only marginally successful in this regard. Indeed, in the friendship study, the opinions of male strangers had no influence at all upon impulsive subjects' judgments of the autokinetic light movement. In addition to resisting advice from others, the findings suggested that impulsive persons were more likely to dominate others. That is, the friendship study of dominance found that impulsive persons stated that they were the persons most likely to make the final decision and have the last word in arguments with their friends.

These findings tie in nicely with the clinical literature which also reports that character-disordered persons are less accepting of influence from others (Cleckley, 1964). The findings also appear consistent with the general theoretical position of Eysenck (1957) who stresses that it is more difficult to modify the behavior of extroverts than that of introverts because of physiological differences between the two groups. Also related are the findings of Zuckerman and Link (1968) with normal subjects, who reported that high scorers on the Sensation-Seeking Scale were less field-dependent than low scorers on the Rod and Frame Test. The Impulsiveness Scale and the Sensation-Seeking Scale intercorrelated .52, as may be recalled. What we seem to be dealing with is a continuum of what may loosely be called character development or structure, in which those veering toward the poorly restrained end are less open to influence from both their physical and social environment.

One other point should be made here. We have used negative-value-laden terms in describing this process, such as resistance to influence and the like. The reader should be aware that the same behaviors could be described in very positive terms such as independence of judgment and resistance to conformity. Presumably in an Asch-type conformity experiment, one could expect impulsive individuals to yield far less often to the majority opinion than would nonimpulsive individuals. No data have been collected on this point, but I would expect a greater number of impulsive than nonimpulsive persons to be nonconforming in political and social activities. That is, not being as bound by conventional values, impulsive persons should be much freer to adopt newer values, whether these values originate from the political left or right. If this proves to be so, I would hasten to add that these extreme political positions should not be viewed as being caused by personality per se. Rather, the rejection of conventional social values may allow the person to see more social problems requiring attention; problems to which the more conventional person is selectively blind by virtue of his adherence to conventional dogma.

Finally, the studies reported here suggested several environmental conditions that were influential in modifying the impulsive individual's behavior. In the leadership study anticipation of punishment from the leader produced conformity; in the peer study the presence of an attractive female changed judgments; and in the verbal conditioning study, the possibility of earning money rapidly produced behavioral changes. In other words, threats, sex, and money appeared to be more potent catalysts for change among impulsive persons than such factors as friendship, obligations to duty, and social praise.

CHAPTER 6

Friendship Relations

Thus far, evidence has shown that impulsive persons were less impression-able than nonimpulsive persons and tended to be dominant in the sense of trying to exercise personal decisions concerning themselves and their friends. In this chapter, findings are presented as to how impulsive and nonimpulsive individuals get along with their friends, over and beyond issues concerned with influence. Basically, our interest was in examining how the core restraining behaviors used to define impulsiveness were manifested in friendship relations. In the first study in this section, data are presented which suggest that impulsive individuals are more gregarious and form cliquish friendship relations. Other studies in this section are concerned with how the sensation-seeking needs of impulsive individuals, as well as their low levels of reactivity to anxiety, are manifested in friendship relations.

Friendship Groupings

Individuals tend to maintain balance or consistency among the compo-nents of their belief systems, as many investigators have found (Festinger, 1957). This tendency to maintain balance has been found by Kogan and Taguiri (1958) to extend to beliefs about the ways in which one's friends get along with each other. Kogan and Taguiri have hypothesized that persons experience psychological discomfort if others they know do not have mutual feelings toward their friends. For example, if person O has two friends, A and B, it would be upsetting to O to learn that A and B dislike each other. To reduce this discomfort, Kogan and Taguiri have suggested that balancing mechanisms are invoked to restore consistency in perceptions of friends' relations with each other, so that friends are seen as liking each other and disliking the enemies of their friends, regardless of the true feelings involved.

We have already found that impulsive individuals are less reactive to situations that produce psychological discomfort. Hence, it was speculated that impulsive individuals would be bothered less than nonimpulsive individuals by the perception that their best friends did not like each other. Translating this hypothesis into operational form, it was predicted that if individuals were asked whether their two best friends liked each other, non-impulsive respondents would answer in the affirmative more often than impulsive respondents would.

In anticipation, results of a study to test this idea were antithetical to those predicted. Impulsive subjects reported more balanced friendship relations than nonimpulsive subjects. Nevertheless, the findings are presented because they appear consistent with subsequent studies in this area. In addition, the findings serve to prepare us for other unexpected findings concerning the friendship relations of impulsive and nonimpulsive individuals.

The procedure involved asking 17 impulsive and 10 nonimpulsive (Impulsiveness Scale) sailors who had completed recruit training within the last 12 months to name their five best friends at recruit training. Sailors were also asked to write the names of the three best friends of each of their five best friends. All sailors were above average in intellectual ability (GCT = 53 or more).

The first analysis was limited to examining the relationship between each sailor's two best friends. Did the sailors believe that their two best friends were mutual good friends? The extent of mutual choice between friends was classified into two categories. Balanced, the sailors stated that their two best friends were friends of each other; Unbalanced, either Friend 1 was listed as a friend of Friend 2, but the reverse was not true, or the two best friends were not listed as friends of each other.

Contrary to expectations, 70% of the impulsive sailors and 20% of the nonimpulsive sailors reported balanced friendship relations ($\overline{X}^2 = 4.61$. $p < .05$, corrected for continuity). In other words, impulsive sailors were more likely than nonimpulsive sailors to state that their two best friends were good friends of one another. Furthermore, impulsive sailors perceived more affection between their two best friends than did nonimpulsive sailors. In response to a question as to how their two best friends got along with each other, 53% of the impulsive sailors and 20% of the nonimpulsive sailors stated that they were the "best of friends" ($p < .10$ by chi-square test).

The above trend was still found when the friendship relations among all five best friends were examined. The data were analyzed in terms of the question of how frequently the sailors stated that their best friends were mutual. This reciprocity score could range from 0 to 15, with a score of 15 indicating a high degree of reciprocity between friends. Nonimpulsive sailors had an average score of 4.5 and impulsive sailors had an average score of 7.8. This difference was significant well beyond the .05 level ($F = 6.90$, df 1/25).

Thus, contrary to prediction, the results revealed that impulsive persons were more likely to state that mutual choice among their friends was higher than it was among nonimpulsive person's friends. If we take these results to actually portray friendship groupings, rather than cognitive states of balance, it would appear that impulsive individuals formed cliquish friendships in which mutual choice and liking for each other was high. When going out in the evening on military passes, one might expect the impulsive sailor to leave with perhaps four or five friends, and the nonimpulsive sailor might leave the military camp with only one other friend, or perhaps alone if his friend were busy. Large groups of friends evoke the picture of more excitement and social stimulation; sensory inputs presumably required more by impulsive than nonimpulsive persons.

Although there is very little in the psychological literature against which to compare these findings, the descriptions by Margaret Mead (1939) of the friendship relations formed by men of the Mundugumor and Arapesh societies appear to be relevant. It may be recalled that in the Mundugumor society, competition aggression and striving for interpersonal dominance was high. Mead has described the Mundugumor's relations with each other as being governed by suspicion and hostility. Friendship relations formed around religious cults. Of interest for the present study is that these cults were organized around the idea of "exclusion and the rights of those who had been initiated to taunt and exclude those who had not been" (Mead, page 181). In other words, the Mundugumor's relationship with others could be described as closed and with a high degree of reciprocal choice, similar to those of the impulsive sailors in the present study.

The Arapesh male was encouraged to hold values almost directly opposite to those held by the Mundugumor male. Mead has described the Arapesh male as having many friends, both within his own age group and with his brothers and cousins. When the Arapesh male became restless, he would usually pay a visit to one friend or another. It would appear from Mead's descriptions that the Arapesh male tended to have friends who were not necessarily mutual. Both Mead's research and the results of the present study suggest a possible relation between the character structure of the individual and the extent to which he enters into closed or open friendship relations.

Personality Similarity and Friendships

One possible explanation for the finding that impulsive individuals are attracted to groups of friends, rather than to solitary friendship relations, is that such groups are more likely to satisfy sensation-seeking needs. If this explanation is true, one might also expect that impulsive individuals would be attracted to persons with personalities similar to their own, or at least with similar sensation-seeking needs. Friendships might "wear thin" if the friends of impulsive persons continually "begged off" party-going and other social activities to pursue more "bookish" ways of enjoying themselves.

Before presenting findings on the similarity of personality between impulsive individuals and their friends, we would like to repeat the views of Wright (1969) concerning the relation between attraction and personality similarity. Wright has pointed out that few personality constructs have comfortably predicted interpersonal attraction. Attempts to explain attraction in terms of such notions as complementarity and similarity of personality have generally proved too simple and unable to accommodate empirical findings. Wright argues cogently that personality variables at best can only provide an explanation for interpersonal attraction by assuming that personality tendencies lead to unique patterning of activities which attract or repel others. Hence, attractions are mediated by activities of others which are correlated with personality, but not limited to a given personality configuration.

Keeping in mind the warning that attractions and personality are probably mediated by activities of mutual interest, the following section presents findings on the extent of similarity in impulsiveness scores between friendship dyads. It may be recalled that the autokinetic study described in chapter 4 involved 15 pairs of impulsive subjects and a like number of nonimpulsive subjects and their friends. From another set of studies (to be reported in this chapter) data on an additional 31 pairs of impulsive and nonimpulsive subjects and their friends were obtained, for a total of 61 dyads in all. All subjects and friends were recruited in the manner described in Chapter 6. Impulsiveness scores of friends were either available from a prior large-scale university testing, or the scales were completed by the friends at the end of the laboratory sessions.

On the average, friends of impulsive subjects had higher impulsiveness scores than friends of nonimpulsive subjects. The average Impulsiveness Index score of friends of impulsive subjects was 35.40 as compared to 28.48 for friends of nonimpulsive subjects. By F test, this difference in scores was significant beyond the .01 level ($F = 8.98$, df 1/59).

Whereas the differences were in the predicted direction, it should be noted that not too many impulsive subjects actually brought impulsive friends to the laboratory. Only 33% of the friends of impulsive subjects could actually be classified as impulsive themselves. Most of these friends were classified as moderate on the Impulsiveness Index. In contrast, 65% of the friends of nonimpulsive subjects could be classified as nonimpulsive. Perhaps it was just more difficult to persuade impulsive friends to come to the laboratory. In any case, this pattern of scores does not fit the prediction that impulsive subjects would have impulsive friends.

A more direct test of the assumption that impulsive individuals are attracted to impulsive friends would involve information involving the extent to which subjects were attracted to friends who were similar to themselves in impulsiveness. Fortunately this information was available for 54 of the dyads in terms of the Friendship Index. It may be recalled that this index was composed of ratings of closeness of friendship on a five-point rating scale, combined with the length of time that the respondent had been a friend of the person with him that day. The higher the Friendship Index score, the greater the feelings of interpersonal attraction between members of the dyad.

Each dyad was classified as to whether the subject and friend were homogeneous or heterogeneous in terms of impulsiveness. Homogeneity was defined as both subject and friend classified as impulsive (N = 7 dyads) or nonimpulsive (N = 17 dyads). Table 18 shows the average Friendship Index scores (subject's plus friend's) for dyads jointly classified in terms of homogeneity–heterogeneity and level of subjects' impulsiveness. It can be observed that homogeneous dyads liked each other more than heterogeneous dyads. This was especially true for impulsive homogeneous dyads.

TABLE 18

INTERPERSONAL ATTRACTION AMONG HOMOGENEOUS AND HETEROGENEOUS DYADS, AS MEASURED BY THE FRIENDSHIP INDEX

Subject	Homogeneous		Heterogeneous	
	$\overline{X}$	N^a	$\overline{X}$	N^a
Impulsive subject and friend	16.14	7	11.00	19
Nonimpulsive subject and friend	12.24	17	11.42	11

^{a} N = dyads.

An analysis of variance of these data yielded a significant F ratio for the composition variable ($F = 5.52$, df $1/50$, $p < .05$), supporting the belief that friends would be more attracted to each other when they had similar impulsiveness scores. However, as suggested above, this relationship was strongest among impulsive subjects. Simple effects tests revealed that a dyad composed of an impulsive subject and an impulsive friend showed more attraction to each other than a dyad composed of an impulsive subject and a moderate or nonimpulsive friend ($p < .01$). Among nonimpulsive dyads, the relationship between attraction and similarity of impulsiveness scores was not significant. Whatever the factors influencing interpersonal liking among nonimpulsive subjects, similarity of impulsiveness was not one of them.

Self-Disclosure

Self-disclosure and the revelation of intimate information about the self has been seen by novelists, poets, and social scientists alike as an affirmation of trust and affection with another person. The extent to which the individual divulges intimate information about himself also has a central role in several theories of interpersonal relations and adjustment (Altman and Haythorn, 1965; Jourard and Lasakow, 1958). Altman, for instance, has proposed that as friendships deepen, the interpersonal exchange proceeds from the superficial to the exchange of more intimate units of information.

With this view of information in mind, we next examined the extent to which impulsive and nonimpulsive persons revealed intimate and highly personal information about themselves to their friends. It was expected that impulsive persons would reveal more intimate information to friends than would nonimpulsive persons. This prediction was based upon previous findings that impulsive persons were more verbal, and more importantly, less reactive to situations producing shame and anxiety. Feelings of anxiety and shame are known restraints against disclosing intimate information about the self. It follows that if impulsive persons were to experience lesser degrees of these restraining emotions, they would then perhaps be more candid and more open about themselves.

The procedure for this investigation involved 12 impulsive and 12 nonimpulsive subjects who brought friends to the laboratory. Subjects and friends completed a questionnaire concerning conversations held with each other. The questionnaire contained 47 statements about various aspects of the self, scaled for degree of intimacy. The items were drawn from a larger pool of 671 items published by Taylor and Altman (1966). These 671 items had been scaled for degree of intimacy using samples of college students and navy-enlisted men as raters. For each item in the present study, respondents were asked to check "true" if they had discussed the statement with their friend.

Of the items used, 23 had scale values indicating high levels of intimacy. It was predicted that impulsive respondents would state that they had discussed more of these intimate items with their friends than would nonimpulsive respondents.

An additional 24 nonintimate items were included in the questionnaire. These nonintimate items were included as a control against such extraneous factors as response-set accounting for the results. It was expected that nonimpulsive subjects would indicate that they had disclosed as many nonintimate items to their friends as impulsive subjects had to their friends.

A sample of intimate and nonintimate items used in the questionnaire are: *Intimate:* "What I daydream about"; "Things in my past I am most ashamed about"; "Things I would usually not reveal to other people." *Nonintimate:* "How often I shave"; "How I like my clothes to fit"; "The ages of my brothers and sisters."

Subjects and friends answered the intimacy questionnaire in separate rooms and were not allowed to discuss their answers with each other. A self-disclosure score for intimate and nonintimate items was obtained by simply summing separately the number of intimate and nonintimate items checked "true."

Closeness of friendship as measured by the Friendship Index was related to the amount of information disclosed. As a control for this, a covariance analysis was used in comparing the self-disclosure scores of impulsive and non-impulsive respondents, with the Friendship Index as the covariate. To increase the number of cases available for analysis, self-disclosure scores of friends who could be classified as impulsive (N = 7) and nonimpulsive (N = 10) were also included in the analysis. This resulted in a 2×2 analysis of covariance, with two levels of impulsiveness as the first factor and whether the respondent was a subject or friend as the second.

Level of impulsiveness was significantly related to the number of intimate items disclosed ($F = 9.12$, df 1/35, $p < .01$). As shown in Table 19, the average number of intimate items revealed was 13.9 for impulsive respondents and 9.6 for nonimpulsive respondents. A similar analysis of the nonintimate items was not significant ($F = 1.60$, df 1/35), suggesting that nonimpulsive persons were not generally inhibited in their conversations, but were only so when topics likely to provoke embarrassment were under discussion. This pattern of differential inhibition of speech according to the degree of anxiety in the situation appears similar to the one found in the previous study of willingness to talk in the classroom.

TABLE 19
AVERAGE NUMBER OF INTIMATE AND NONINTIMATE ITEMS DISCLOSED[a]

| | Impulsive | | Nonimpulsive | |
	Subjects (N = 12)	Friends (N = 7)	Subjects (N = 12)	Friends (N = 10)
Intimate items	13.9	13.8	10.7	8.3
Nonintimate items	17.1	15.7	15.2	14.1

[a] Averages adjusted for Friendship Index.

Social Activities

Another question investigated was how frequently impulsive and non-impulsive persons socialized with their friends. We were interested in this question as part of the contention about stimulation-seeking needs among impulsive and nonimpulsive individuals. Translating these needs into behaviors would lead to the prediction that impulsive persons should be more socially active and should operate upon their environment more frequently as a means of "stirring up excitement."

This question was tested by having 15 impulsive and 15 nonimpulsive subjects and their friends separately fill out a questionnaire concerned with the number of activities they jointly carried out. These subjects and friends were the same as those used in the autokinetic study.

Five joint activities that involved spending time together were described in the questionnaire as follows: double dating; going to sports events; playing cards or going to the movies; going to social affairs; studying together. Each item asked how frequently respondents engaged in this activity with the friend who was with them that day. Answers were on a 9-point scale ranging from "rarely" to "all the time." Scores were summed over the five items to give a total activity score for each respondent.

Once again it was found that closeness of friendship influenced the relationship between friends, with fewer reports of joint activities made by acquaintances than by good friends. Therefore, in the analysis, respondents were dichotomized at the median of the Friendship Index. Among acquaintances there was no significant difference between impulsive subjects and nonimpulsive subjects in the extent of activities with their friends. Among good friends however, impulsive subjects had significantly higher ($p < .05$) activity scores than nonimpulsive subjects. These findings were also examined by adding subjects' and friends' activity scores together to obtain a combined estimate of extent of socializing. This analysis yielded similar significant results ($p < .02$). In short, among good friends, more time was spent by impulsive subjects socializing with their friends than was spent by nonimpulsive subjects.

The Influence of Time upon Friendship Relations

It has been reiterated that closeness of friendship influenced the various dependent measures studied. This, of course, is not too surprising. As friendships deepen one can expect friends to engage in more activities together and to reveal more intimate information about themselves. However, an unexpected finding was that closeness of friendship affected the dependent measures differentially for impulsive and nonimpulsive subjects. In general, the findings suggested that the process of friendship occurred in a more orderly and predictable manner among impulsive persons than non-impulsive persons.

The first instance in which these differential relations were noted was in the relation between the number of months respondents stated they had been friends with the person with them at the laboratory and subjects' ratings of how much they liked this person. From the general literature on interpersonal attraction it could be expected that the longer the period of friendship, the higher their ratings of closeness (Festinger, Schachter and Back, 1950; Guilford, 1954, page 295).

This expectation was tested in the present study by computing the correlation between the number of months each respondent said he had been friends with the person with him that day and each respondent's rating of closeness of friendship. The correlation was based upon a total of 106 subjects and friends from both the study of interpersonal influence and the study on self-disclosure. In addition, separate correlations were computed for subjects and friends classified as impulsive (26 subjects and 10 friends), friends classified as in the middle third of the impulsiveness index ($N = 20$), and subjects and friends classified as nonimpulsive (27 subjects and 24 friends).

Overall the correlation between months of friendship and ratings of closeness of friendship was .43 ($p < .01$). However, the correlation between these two indices of friendship was strongest for impulsive subjects ($r = .67$, $p < .01$), next for moderately impulsive respondents ($r = 46$, $p < .05$), and lowest for nonimpulsive respondents ($r = .27$, $p < .10$). The difference between the correlations for impulsive and nonimpulsive respondents was significant beyond the .05 level, by Fisher's Z' transformation. Almost exactly equivalent correlations of .64 ($p < .05$) and .27 (p ns) were obtained when only the responses of impulsive and nonimpulsive subjects were analyzed.

It is evident, then, that time per se only weakly influenced the degree of interpersonal attraction for those classified as nonimpulsive. These individuals appeared almost as likely to regard as close friends persons known for a short period as persons known for a longer period of time. Impulsive individuals, on the other hand, more closely approximated the predicted fit between time and interpersonal liking. The longer they knew a person, the more likely they were to regard him as a good friend.

The second instance in which closeness of friendship differentially mediated the friendship behavior of impulsive and nonimpulsive persons was in terms of the amount of information revealed about the self. Table 20 shows the correlation between the number of intimate and nonintimate items revealed and the three measures of friendship (time, ratings, and time + ratings). These correlations are shown for the total sample of 48 respondents who completed the intimacy questionnaire, and separately for impulsive and nonimpulsive respondents.

TABLE 20

PRODUCT–MOMENT CORRELATIONS BETWEEN FRIENDSHIP INDICES AND NUMBER OF
INTIMATE AND NONINTIMATE ITEMS DISCUSSED WITH FRIENDS

Items and indices	Impulsive (N = 18)	Nonimpulsive (N = 22)	Total (N = 48)
Intimate items and:			
1. Months of friendship	.59[b]	.33	.45[b]
2. Ratings of closeness of friendship	.72[b]	.28	.40[b]
3. Friendship Index (1+2)	.73[b]	.36	.51[b]
Nonintimate items and:			
1. Months of friendship	.34	.12	.25
2. Ratings of closeness of friendship	.39	.11	.24
3. Friendship Index (1 + 2)	.40	.13	.28

[a] Total includes eight friends classified in the middle third of impulsiveness.
[b] $p < .01$.

For the total sample, all measures of friendship were significantly correlated with the number of intimate items revealed, but were not significantly correlated with the number of nonintimate items revealed. These findings are consistent with a social penetration theory of Altman's (Altman and Haythorn, 1965) which predicted that as friendships deepened, more intimate information about the self would be revealed to one's friends.

It may also be observed in Table 20 that the relationship between closeness of friendship and self-disclosure was strongest among impulsive

70   6. FRIENDSHIP RELATIONS

respondents. For instance, the Friendship Index correlated .73 with number
of intimate items disclosed among impulsive respondents and .36 among
nonimpulsive respondents. While depth of friendship appeared to be a
primary determinant of the extent to which impulsive respondents discussed
intimate details of their lives, depth of friendship was much less of a determinant among nonimpulsive respondents. Taken together, the findings
revealed that nonimpulsive respondents disclosed relatively little about
themselves and the rate of self-disclosure increased at a very slow rate, even
among good friends.

A third instance in which depth of friendship differentially influenced
impulsive and nonimpulsive subjects behavior was in terms of their joint
activities. Closeness of friendship was related to the extent that impulsive
subjects reported socializing with their friends. This relationship was not as
strong for nonimpulsive subjects. For impulsive subjects, the Friendship
Index correlated significantly ($rho = .60$, $p < .05$) with Activity Scores. The
relationship between the Friendship Index and Activity Scores was not
significant, though positive, for nonimpulsive subjects ($p = .34$, p ns).
Although these correlations were not significantly different from each other,
they were consistent with the previous findings concerning depth of friendship. In the present example, it would appear that impulsive persons sharply
increased in amount of time spent socializing with another person as their
feelings of friendship for this person increased. These increases in socializing
were less noticeable among nonimpulsive persons.

A fourth instance in which depth of friendship differentially influenced
impulsive and nonimpulsive subjects involved attempts to dominate. It may
be recalled that dominating behavior between members of a dyad was
investigated in terms of a ten-item questionnaire concerned with such items
as "making the final decision in a disagreement," "being the one who
suggests places to go," etc. (see Chapter 4). The findings revealed that

TABLE 21

CORRELATION BETWEEN FRIENDSHIP MEASURES AND QUESTIONNAIRE
MEASURES OF INTERPERSONAL DOMINANCE

Measure of friendship	Impulsive (N = 15)	Nonimpulsive (N = 15)
Length of friendship	.57[a]	.21
Rating of Friendship	.69[a]	.09
Friendship Index	.62[a]	.17

[a] $p < .01$.

among good friends, impulsive subjects had higher dominance scores than nonimpulsive subjects. It was also found, as shown in Table 21, that depth of friendship was differentially correlated with dominance behavior.

For impulsive subjects there were moderately strong correlations between dominance and friendship, ranging from .57 to .69. For nonimpulsive subjects these correlations were not significant, although still positive (r's from .09 to .21). Impulsive subjects reported dominance over their friends according to their strength of friendship. This relation did not hold among nonimpulsive subjects.

Summary

The findings helped clarify the ways in which behaviors associated with impulsiveness affect friendship relations. It was found that impulsive persons revealed more intimate information about themselves to friends and engaged in more social activities with them, than did nonimpulsive persons. Impulsive persons also appeared to have more friends in common and liked those friends best who had similar personality structures. Presumably these differences in interaction are manifestations of differences between impulsive and nonimpulsive persons in their responses to anxiety-provoking stimuli and in their needs for excitement and sensory stimulation.

The lack of orderly and predictable friendship relations among nonimpulsive persons is puzzling and deserves comment. The process of friendship and interpersonal attraction is known to be facilitated by such factors as the duration of acquaintance (Guilford, 1954), the perception of similarity in personality and attitudes (Byrne, 1961; D. M. Kipnis, 1962), and by mutual exchange of information (Newcomb, 1961; Altman and Haythorn, 1965). These processes were revealed most clearly for impulsive persons. As friendships deepened, impulsive persons revealed more intimate information about themselves, engaged in more activities with their friends, and reported more attempts to dominate their friends. This last finding was unexpected, but is perhaps consistent with the basic behaviors of impulsive persons. That is, within the context of genuine attraction and friendship, more bickering and arguments over dominance matters may be tolerated. On the other hand, the friendship relations of nonimpulsive persons were much less predictable in terms of these general processes. Frequently a nonimpulsive person would bring in a person he had known for perhaps three months and state that this was his best friend. Or he would report that he had engaged in few activities with a best friend whom he had known for almost five years. He also disclosed few intimate details about himself to his friends. The only clear-cut effect of friendship for nonimpulsive persons, as reported in Chapter 4, was that close friends were more likely than acquaintances to influence their judgments.

The picture presented then of nonimpulsive persons is that they appear guarded and inhibited in their friendship relations. In fact, their behavior closely approximates the description given by Eysenck (1964) of the introvert as a solitary person, who basically does not enjoy interactions with others. The reason for these solitary preferences, however, are not clear. One may conjecture, however, following Zajonc (1965), that interaction with other persons may be a greater source of arousal or stress for nonimpulsive than impulsive persons. This high level of stress in turn makes the individual appear more "gauche" in his relations with others and also inhibits the learning of social skills.

The findings also raise the question of whether differences exist in the functional values placed upon friendship by impulsive and nonimpulsive persons. That is, are they seeking different satisfactions from commerce with their friends? Wright (1969) points out that friendship means different things to different people with respect to the advantages or benefits of such a relationship. He goes on to say that two persons may differ widely on the kinds of rewards they desire from others. Unfortunately, the activity questionnaire used in our research did not sample a large enough range of behaviors to reveal such differences. Recently, several authors have described schemes for classifying interpersonal relations (Bennis *et al.*, 1968; page 650; Wright, 1969) which suggest the direction that future research might take in investigating this question. Wright (1969), for example, has developed a questionnaire to measure three functional values that persons may seek from friendship relations. Stimulation value: the degree to which the individual finds another as interesting and imaginative, capable of introducing the subject to new ideas and the like; utility value: the degree to which the subject sees another as cooperative, helpful, and generally willing to use his resources to help the subject meet his own personal goals and needs; and ego support value: the degree to which the subject sees another person as encouraging, supportive, nonthreatening, and concerned with his comfort.

Perhaps impulsive persons are seeking friendships that yield utility value, insofar as they use others to satisfy personal aspirations. Furthermore, borrowing from the classification scheme of Bennis *et al.*, impulsive persons appear to seek friendships that satisfy emotional-expressive needs. That is, they appear to seek out others who can help them satisfy sensation-seeking needs. At the present time, it is not at all clear as to where nonimpulsive persons would fit within these classification systems. Further research is most obviously called for.

CHAPTER 7

Exploitive Behaviors

It seems to be true that the more characterologically disturbed the individual, the less frequently he experiences psychological stress and discomfort, and the more frequently persons close to him have unpleasant experiences. That is, individuals fixated at earlier stages of character development manifest this fixation most directly in their interpersonal relations. The life history of psychopaths usually reveals conflicts with peers, parents, and school or civil authority. Loevinger (1966) has described persons who were fixated at earlier stages of ego development as exploitive in their dealings with others. Loevinger states that at these stages, the individual's personal preoccupations are with "control and advantage, deception, getting the better of, and so on. Life is a zero-sum game; what you win, I lose" (page 199).

We undertook three studies investigating exploitive behavior among impulsive and nonimpulsive individuals. In these studies, the prisoner's dilemma game was used as the procedure to study exploitation. Throughout, subjects were allowed to control the amount of money that could be earned by their opponents and themselves. We were interested in the extent to which subjects would share money with the person they were paired with by accepting a lesser amount of money for themselves, or would take a greater amount of money for themselves, leaving less for the other person. Furthermore, we were interested in studying conditions that influenced impulsive and nonimpulsive persons to share money with others, or to keep

73

it for themselves. Two conditions reported upon here were the dependency of the opponent and the opponent's control of retaliatory powers.

Description of the Prisoner's Dilemma Game

The basic prisoner's dilemma game, as described by Swingle (1968) is a two-person, two-choice situation, which is designed so that either person's payoff is determined by both their behavior. An example is given in the accompanying matrix, where players A and B are each provided with two alternative responses, response 1 and response 2. The rules of the game are quite simple. On any particular trial, each player must decide whether he wants to play response 1 or 2. Each player usually makes his decision without knowledge of his partner's choice and then the experimenter announces the results of the trial. The payoffs for player A are shown in the left-hand corner of each quadrant and those for B are shown in the right-hand corner. It can be seen that if on a given trial, A chooses response 1 and B also chooses response 1, the players will win 12¢ each. However, if player A chooses response 1 and B chooses response 2, A will win nothing and B will win 18¢. If both players choose response 2, then they will only earn 6¢ each.

	Player B	
	Response 1	Response 2
Player A		
Response 1	12¢, 12¢	0¢, 18¢
Response 2	18¢, 0¢	6¢, 6¢

Thus, if A and B cooperate and trust each other enough to choose response 1, they will both make 12c. Response 1 may be called a co-operative and trusting response. Response 1 is cooperative because it does not penalize the other player. It also makes larger rewards available to the other player than response 2 does. Response 1 is also a trusting response because the person is taking some degree of risk that his cooperative response will be exploited rather than reciprocated and that he will receive no reward at all. In effect, the person is trusting the other person not to make a number 2 response.

In our studies the above procedures were used, with one major exception. This was that subjects played against a simulated player, who almost always chose the trusting response. In addition, knowledge of this choice was conveyed to the subject before he made his decision. Thus the subject could decide to be cooperative in return and share money by choosing response

1, or he could exploit the other player by choosing response 2, giving himself a large payoff and the other player less.

EXPLORATORY STUDY

The first study was exploratory, designed to see whether impulsive individuals would exploit others, under the conditions described above.

Navy enlisted men played the Prisoner's Dilemma game against a fictitious sailor. The game was explained to them as a study in decision making. Subjects were told that they were paired with another sailor, whom they would not meet. The payoff matrix (as shown on page 74) ranged from zero cents to 18¢, depending upon the joint choices of both persons playing. Two cooperative choices yielded 12¢ for each subject; one cooperative and one noncooperative choice yielded 0¢ and 18¢, and two noncooperative choices yielded 6¢ each.

By means of a rigged toss, it was always arranged that the fictitious sailor would choose first on each of the 12 trials in the game. Subjects were told the number of trials to be played. In addition, the results of the fictitious sailor's choice were communicated to the subject before he made his choice. Within the limits of the game this allowed the subject to control the outcome for the fictitious sailor. The experimenter, playing the role of the fictitious sailor, adopted a modified cooperative role and always chose response 1 as long as the subject made a similar choice. If the subject chose response 2 (thus giving himself 18¢ and the fictitious sailor nothing), for the next two plays the experimenter chose response 2, and then reverted to response 1. There were a total of 18 subjects in all; 6 were nonimpulsive and 12 were impulsive. All had GCT scores of 51 or better. The dependent measure was the number of response-1 choices (cooperative choices) made by each subject over the 12 trials.

The average number of cooperative choices made by impulsive subjects was 3.46. Nonimpulsive subjects made 7.18 cooperative choices. Analysis of variance of these data yielded an F ratio that did not reach customary levels of significance ($F = 3.14$, df 1/16, $p < .15$). On the last trial, in which all subjects were given a cooperative choice, 2 of the 12 impulsive and 4 of the 6 nonimpulsive subjects made cooperative choices. By Fisher's exact test, these differences in cooperative choices did not exceed the .05 level. Although the findings were in the expected direction, they were not particularly conclusive.

DEPENDENCY OF THE OPPONENT

In the next study, taken from a Ph.D thesis by Peter Jenkins (1968), an attempt was made to correct several of the weaknesses in the first study.

First of all, a larger number of subjects was used. In addition, the first study punished exploitive behavior by the fact that the fictitious sailor immediately reverted to a noncooperative style of play when the subject became noncooperative. Over time, this systematic noncooperative response by the fictitious sailor lost money for the subject (he made only 6¢, rather than 12¢ during these trials). In Jenkin's study, the subject was given a greater opportunity to exploit the other player without loss to himself. This was accomplished by having the fictitious player make uncooperative choices on 13 of the 16 trials played, regardless of the subject's level of cooperation. On trials 3, 8, and 13, the fictitious player made uncooperative choices. This produced a game that was highly cooperative and yet realistic from the subject's point of view. In initial pilot work, it was found that to have played a totally cooperative game would have lacked realism as far as the subjects were concerned.

Jenkin's was also concerned with how the fictitious person was perceived by subjects. He predicted that impulsive persons would be more exploitive with a weak and submissive player than with a strong and dominant one. This prediction was based upon the assumption that the expression of such socially condemned behavior as exploitation would vary among impulsive individuals as a function of the restraining forces in the environment. To the extent that these forces were high, impulsive persons should inhibit tendencies to take all the money from the other player. In terms of the present study, the perception of weakness and dependency in the other player by impulsive persons was predicted to lead to the cognition that it would be possible to maximize one's winnings without concern about possible retaliation. Contrarily, Jenkins predicted that the perception of weakness and dependency in the other player should more readily activate the internalized norm of social responsibility (Berkowitz and Daniels 1964) among nonimpulsive subjects and make them more cooperative. Berkowitz has suggested that many middle class university students feel obligated to help people who are dependent on them. However this helping behavior appears contingent upon the activation of a norm of social responsibility. In Berkowitz's terms, it was expected that this norm of social responsibility could be more easily invoked by dependency cues among nonimpulsive than impulsive subjects.

Experimental variations in the dependency of the fictitious player were created by using three different roles: a self-sufficient authority figure, a fellow student of reasonable independence, and a dependent fellow student. Paired with each of these roles were 10 impulsive and 10 nonimpulsive university students. The Impulsiveness Index was used to classify students; all had SAT scores of 1000 or more.

The differential perceptions of the fictitious player were created by having the subject and fictitious player describe themselves to each other via microphones before beginning play. (Subjects were told they would not meet the other player who was presumably located in another room.) The self-descriptions were based upon an outline which asked the subject to describe his hobbies, college major, dating frequency, and the like.

The authority figure described himself as an ex-marine graduate student, who liked to box, was studying law, had strong religious affiliations, and was reasonably independent. The tape recording used went as follows:

> I'm older than you, Man B. School—well, it's a long story. I went to South Philly High School—then I came here, uh, for a degree in Political Science, played a little football while I was here. Let's see—hobbies—umm-well, I still like to box and one night a week I coach for the police athletic league. I date fairly often, just about every weekend. I met my future wife at a church—uh—we generally go to church-sponsored parties; uhm, well after school I joined the Marines; I was a physical training instructor at Campe Lejeune. Then after the Marines I was with the Police Department here until September and then I got accepted to law school, and that's why I came back here. Let's see—future goals; well, I went to finish here, of course, and then I'd like to get a job with the District Attorney's office.

The peer was portrayed as a fun-loving college undergraduate.

> I'm the same age as you, Man B. I went to high school in Media, out in Delaware County. Now I'm a Bio major here at Temple, but I'm not sure what I want to do. Uh, I played some basketball in high school and I still follow sports, go to a ball game once in a while. Dates—yeah; I go out with girls when I'm not studying. Umm, what do I like to do on dates? Oh, ya know, dance, or movies, or uh anything else I can get. That's all I have to say about dates. Kinds of jobs? Well I did, uh, the usual summer jobs, you know, waiting on tables, camp counselor, a couple of years. Uhm, future goals? Well, when I get out of here I'm going to eat. That's about all I have to say, except I'm not too sure what I want to do.

The dependent peer was portrayed as a poor, hardworking student, who supported himself and spent all his spare time either studying or earning money and longed for some time and money to enjoy life.

> I'm the same age as you, Man B. I went to South Philly High School; I played basketball, umm, 'til my father got sick, and now I have to work. Let's see—interests, umm, dates—well, ya know—this may sound stupid, but I just don't have time; I have to work like hell to stay in school. Jobs —well, I'm here in a Work Studies Program. That's the kind of job I have now. The only other thing is a goal. Hmm, some day I'd like to be a CPA and I'd also like to own a nice car.

To assess the effectiveness of these presentations, each subject described his partner prior to the actual game, by choosing 10 adjectives from a 35-item list of adjectives. In the authority condition subjects described the simulated player most frequently ($p < .05$) as strong, sociable, ambitious, energetic, firm, confident, and aggressive. The peer was seen significantly more often as being contented, sociable, fun-loving, sympathetic, and shy. The dependent peer was described as lonely, sensitive, sympathetic, shy, and firm.

Results

Each subject played two games of 16 trials each with the simulated player. The first game (Low Payoff) had a payoff matrix ranging from 0¢ to 4¢. The second game had a payoff matrix ranging from 0¢ to 18¢. Based upon prior findings concerning the materialistic orientation of impulsive subjects, Jenkins had predicted that impulsive subjects would make fewer cooperative responses when playing in the High Payoff than in the Low Payoff game. That is, as the amount of money increased, impulsive persons would be less willing to share it. Payoff order was counterbalanced within each condition.

Table 22 shows the average number of cooperative choices made by subjects in the Low Payoff and in the High Payoff games. In both instances, there was little difference between impulsive and nonimpulsive subjects, except in the number of cooperative responses made when paired with the dependent peer. An analysis of variance of the Low Payoff game found a significant interaction between impulsiveness and the other player's role ($F = 3.29$, df 2/54, $p < .05$). A similar analysis of the High Payoff game found a significant main effect for the factor of impulsiveness ($F = 4.04$, df 1/54, $p < .05$).

TABLE 22

COOPERATIVE CHOICES IN THE PRISONER'S DILEMMA GAME

Simulated player's role	Low payoff		High payoff	
	Impulsive $\bar{X}$	Nonimpulsive $\bar{X}$	Impulsive $\bar{X}$	Nonimpulsive $\bar{X}$
Authority	8.3	5.6	6.0	5.2
Peer	5.8	8.9	5.9	8.7
Dependent peer	5.7	9.8	5.2	10.6

Simple effects tests of both the High Payoff and Low Payoff games revealed that nonimpulsive subjects were more cooperative than impulsive subjects when paired with the Dependent Peer ($p < .05$). The difference in sharing behavior between impulsive and nonimpulsive subjects was not significant for the Peer and Authority roles.

Jenkins originally proposed that impulsive persons would be more cooperative with a less dependent than with a more dependent person. This hypothesis was not supported. Whereas impulsive persons did play a slightly more cooperative game with the authority role than with the dependent peer, these differences were not statistically significant. Furthermore, the amount of money involved in the games had no influence upon impulsive persons' play. It can be seen in Table 22 that both the impulsive and nonimpulsive person's level of sharing remained fairly constant from the Low to High Payoff games.

The primary reason for the significant differences in cooperative play was the fact that nonimpulsive players increased the number of their cooperative responses when paired with the dependent peer. In both games, the non-impulsive player was significantly more cooperative toward the dependent peer than toward the authority figure ($p < .05$). This finding appears consistent with the assumption that sympathy for the dependent peer would activate an internalized norm of social responsibility among nonimpulsive players. This feeling of responsibility then inducing a more cooperative and less exploitive style of play. The necessity for invoking internalized norms as the mediating mechanism is indicated by the fact that nonimpulsive subjects were not particularly cooperative when paired with the authority figure. Presumably the authority figure was viewed as self-sufficient, and not in any need of special assistance. Thus he was "fair game" for anyone.

At a more general level the findings are also consistent with the view that impulsive persons are less open to social influence from others. In the present instance, the pressure for change in behavior originated from the dependent peer, whose implicit request for sympathy and money changed the amount of sharing behavior of nonimpulsive subjects in the direction advocated by the appeal, but did not alter impulsive subject's behavior.

Location of Restraining Forces

Once a person has been instigated to carry out some socially undesirable act, there are at least two reasons why he may fail to carry out the act. On the one hand he may possess strong inner convictions that restrain him. That is, no matter how much he is tempted, he knows the behavior is wrong and therefore does not do it. On the other hand, the person may perceive that the environment contains forces capable of punishing him if he carries out the act. Once again, the act is not carried out, but this time the reasons reside in concerns over retribution from some outside agency. For most persons, of course, the inhibition of a socially prohibited act is the result of a combination of internalized and external restraining forces. Furthermore, the weight given to these sources of restraint will vary from situation to situation, depending upon the strength of instigation, the nature of the act, and so on. Nevertheless, for purposes of experimental analysis it is useful to exaggerate the differences between these two sources of restraint.

From what has already been written, we would expect impulsive persons to exhibit some socially disapproved behavior when the social setting contained no restraining forces, and to inhibit this behavior when external restraining forces were present. In the previous study, Jenkins attempted to test this statement by varying external restraining forces in terms of the personal strength and dominance of the "other player." At best, this manipulation had very little influence upon the exploitive behavior of impulsive persons. Actually, Jenkins' simulated players could not retaliate for subjects' exploitive play. The subjects were told that they would not meet the ex-marine and amateur boxer at the end of the experiment in order to discuss how they played. Had this expectation been aroused, perhaps they would have been more cautious in their manner of playing. As the situation stood, however, subjects knew that they were not to meet their opponents and hence did not need to concern themselves over justifying the nature of their play with a possibly angry ex-boxer.

In the next study, the strength of environmental restraining forces was more directly studied (Goodstadt and Kipnis). Rather than potential physical retaliation, the restraining force consisted of variations in the extent to which the "other player" could control the amount of money earned by subjects in the Prisoner's Dilemma Game. The prediction was that when the simulated "other player's" powers to retaliate for exploitive behavior were weak, impulsive subjects would be noncooperative. As the other player's retaliatory powers increased, it was further predicted that the noncooperative play of the impulsive players would decrease.

PROCEDURE

As in the previous studies, the basic form of the prisoner's dilemma game was modified in that subjects played against a fictitious player. The subjects were told that they would not meet the other player either during or after the game. They were also told that there would be two separate bargaining games of 16 trials each, and that they could keep the money earned at the end of both games. A cooperative set was used by including in the instructions a discussion that stressed that successful bargaining procedures usually resulted in satisfaction with the outcome for both parties.

Only the first game of 16 trials was actually played. The payoffs used are shown in Table 23 under the heading of First Game Payoffs. The first entry of each call refers to the amount of money won by the fictitious player and the second entry refers to the amount won by the subject. As in the other studies, the fictitious player chose first on each trial and his decision was relayed by electric signal to the subject before he had to make his choice. The fictitious student played cooperatively, choosing response 1 on 14 of the 16 trials. This allowed subjects to either adopt a cooperative set and share with the other player, or a noncooperative set in which the subject took all the money for himself.

To give the subjects the expectation that the fictitious player would have control over the money won in the second game, subjects were told that the fictitious player would be given his turn to choose last on each trial of the second game. Subjects were also told that their decisions would be relayed to the fictitious player.

TABLE 23

PAYOFFS USED IN THE PRISONER'S DILEMMA GAME

First game

| | | Fictitious student's choice | |
	Subject's choice	Response 1	Response 2
	Response 1	12¢, 12¢	18¢, 0¢
	Response 2	0¢, 18¢	6¢, 6¢

Proposed second game

| | Weak power game | | Equal power game | | Strong power game | |
| | Confederate's choice | | Confederate's choice | | Confederate's choice | |
Subject's choice	Response 1	Response 2	Response 1	Response 2	Response 1	Response 2
Response 1	2¢, 2¢	3¢, 0¢	12¢, 12¢	18¢, 10¢	12¢, 12¢	12¢, −20¢
Response 2	0¢, 3¢	1¢, 1¢	0¢, 18¢	6¢, 6¢	18¢, 18¢	18¢, −24¢

Variations in the Retaliatory powers of the fictitious student were introduced by varying the amount of money he controlled in the second game. Three payoff matrices were used, as shown in Table 23 under the heading of Proposed Second Game. For subjects in the Weak Power Condition, the range of money controlled by the fictitious student was minimal, ranging from 0¢ to 3¢. Thus, subjects in this condition could maximise their winnings in the first game without being too concerned about the amount of money won or lost in the second game.

For subjects in the Equal Power condition, the range of payoffs controlled by the fictitious player was equal to those controlled by the subjects in the first game. In the Strong Power condition, the subjects could either win up to 18¢ per trial or have up to 24¢ per trial subtracted from their prior winnings, depending upon the decision of the fictitious player. For instance, if the subject chose response 1, the fictitious player could chose response 1 in return, giving each player 12¢ apiece. Or the fictitious player could chose response 2, giving himself 12¢, but causing 20¢ to be subtracted from the earnings of the subject.

The subjects were given knowledge of the retaliatory powers controlled by the fictitious player by requiring all students to play two practice trials from each game, at the beginning of the experimental session. At the completion of the first game, the subjects filled out a questionnaire as to who they believed controlled the total amount of money that could be won.

The participants of this study consisted of 36 impulsive and 36 non-impulsive students (classified on the basis of the Impulsiveness Index) with SAT scores greater than 1000. To each of the three power conditions, 12 impulsive and 12 nonimpulsive students were randomly assigned.

The analysis of the data consisted of dividing subjects at the median of their cooperative or 1 responses (6 or less) into those who shared with the fictitious player (given a score of 1) and those who did not share (given a score of 0). This score of 1 or 0 was used as the dependent measure in a 3×2 analysis of variance, with two levels of impulsiveness and three levels of retaliatory power as the independent factors.

Results

Who controlled the total amount of earnings that both persons could earn? In response to the questionnaire items covering this query, 91% of the subjects in the Weak Power condition stated they were in control, 71% of the subjects in the Equal Power condition stated that power was equally shared, and 71% of the subjects in the Strong Power condition stated that the other player controlled the outcomes of earnings. The study was thus only moderately successful in manipulating subjects' perception of the locus of control.

Another indication of the effectiveness of the manipulations came from subjects' self-reports concerning the difficulty they had in reaching a decision as to which choice to make. Difficulty in decision-making in this instance was taken to reflect a conflict between the desire to take all the money and the social norm of sharing with the other player. One could expect subjects to experience the greatest difficulty in decision-making in the Weak Power condition, for it is in this condition that they had the greatest freedom to choose without fear of retribution from the other player. Their only restraint against taking all the money was their consciences. By the same logic, the Strong Power condition should evoke the least difficulty in decision-making, since subjects had the least freedom of choice presented here. In this latter condition, if they were not cooperative in the first game, it was clear that the other player could retaliate by completing wiping out their earnings in the second game.

Table 24 gives the proportions of subjects in each condition who stated on the postgame questionnaire that they experienced "no difficulty" in reaching decisions as to how to play the first game.

TABLE 24

PROPORTIONS OF SUBJECTS WHO STATED THEY EXPERIENCED
"NO DIFFICULTY" IN DECIDING WHICH RESPONSE TO CHOOSE[a]

Experimental condition	Impulsive (%)	Nonimpulsive (%)
Weak Power	67	16
Equal Power	58	42
Strong Power	67	75

[a] N = 12 subjects per cell.

According to experimental conditions, there were no differences in the numbers of impulsive subjects who stated they had "no difficulty" in decision-making. The majority stated that their decisions were made without difficulty. However, there were marked variations according to experimental condition in this regard among nonimpulsive subjects. In the Weak Power condition 84% of the nonimpulsive subjects stated that they experienced difficulties in deciding which response to choose. This number is significantly larger than the corresponding number of impulsive subjects ($p < .05$ by chi-square test) and also significantly higher than the numbers of non-impulsive students who experienced difficulty in decision-making in the Strong Power condition ($p < .05$, by chi-square test). We take these differences among nonimpulsive subjects to reflect a conflict between a desire to maximise monetary gains and an inner concern over the fairness of taking money from a weak opponent who had no chance to retaliate.

The results of the study are summarized in Table 25 which presents the proportion of subjects under each condition who shared with the fictitious player during the play of the first game. These findings are given for the total sample and for a purified subsample of subjects who correctly stated on the postexperimental questionnaire the power relations as structured by the experimenter, i.e., that in the Weak Power condition they had total control, in the Equal Power condition they had equal control, and in the Strong Power condition that the other player had total control.

It may be seen that under conditions of Weak and Equal Power, fewer impulsive than nonimpulsive subjects shared with the fictitious player. However in the Strong Power condition, there was essentially no difference in the proportions of sharing. These outcomes confirm the direction originally specified.

TABLE 25

PROPORTIONS OF SUBJECTS WHO SHARED WITH THE FICTITIOUS PLAYER
(First game)

Experimental condition	Total sample				Purified sample			
	Impulsive		Nonimpulsive		Impulsive		Nonimpulsive	
	%	N	%	N	%	N	%	N
Weak Power	33	12	67	12	27	11	73	11
Equal Power	42	12	67	12	25	8	56	9
Strong Power	67	12	75	12	75	8	78	9

Whereas the trends were in the expected direction, the analysis of variance revealed that in the total sample only the factor of impulsiveness approached significance ($F = 3.94$, df $1/62$, $p < .10$). The analysis of variance of the "purified" sample, however, did yield a significant F ratio for impulsiveness ($F = 4.42$, df $1/50$, $p < .05$).

Several points are of interest in Table 25. First of all, it may be observed that nonimpulsive subjects maintained pretty much the same level of cooperative play over the three experimental conditions. Despite the freedom to take more money that existed in the Weak Power condition, nonimpulsive subjects behaved at about the same level as in the Strong Power condition. We may conclude then that the restraining conditions do not influence the sharing behavior of these individuals.

On the other hand, the sharing behavior of impulsive subjects was influenced by the restraining conditions. The number of impulsive subjects who shared more than doubled from the Weak to Strong Power conditions. For the total sample the increases in cooperative behavior among impulsive subjects was significant at the .10 level, and was significant beyond the .05 level for the "purified" sample.

These findings appear consistent, albeit at a rather weak level, statistically speaking, with the idea that externalized forces are more likely to influence normative behaviors among impulsive persons than nonimpulsive persons. The findings are also consistent with other instances noted elsewhere in this volume, where external pressures were important in inducing impulsive persons to accept conventional social norms. It may be recalled that the performance of impulsive sailors was improved by working for a leader who controlled punitive powers. Their classroom attendance also improved when instructors took daily roll-call.

Summary

The findings of this chapter suggest that impulsive persons are more likely to make decisions that maximize their monetary returns, even if these decisions result in a loss for other persons. Whereas we originally began our discussion in terms of exploitive behaviors, some may argue as to whether the behavior observed in this chapter could be called exploitive. Certainly we found no evidence that impulsive subjects had any great urge to psychologically diminish the other players. In a business context, the behavior shown by impulsive persons would be labeled as shrewd and reasonable, whereas the actions of nonimpulsive persons would be considered as reflecting poor judgment.

Furthermore, nonimpulsive persons also showed a fair amount of non-cooperative behavior. These findings suggest that it may be an over-simplification to expect nonimpulsive persons to consistently act the role of the "good guys," and the impulsive persons to play the role of the "bad guys." Both groups will apparently attempt to maximize their gains with some zeal, if there are not contrary indications against this behavior.

Where nonimpulsive persons appear to differ from impulsive persons is in their responsiveness to environmental cues concerning the fairness of this "taking" behavior. When the cues suggest that noncooperative behavior is unfair or violating social norms, nonimpulsive persons appear to be more responsive to these cues and become cooperative, whereas impulsive persons appear less sensitized to such cues. When such cues are minimal, the differences between impulsive and nonimpulsive persons in this regard tend to disappear. Jenkins' study most clearly illustrated this point. Nonimpulsive subjects responded to the dependent peer by sharing money with him, but they were considerably less willing to share with the authority figure, who presumably could take care of his own interests. Furthermore, it is quite possible that if the needs of the dependent peer were made stronger and more obvious, the impulsive person's "norm of responsibility" would also have been activated and they too would have shown increased cooperation.

Basically the argument that is advanced here is that the differences between impulsive and nonimpulsive persons with regard to cooperative behavior resides in the fact that impulsive persons appear more sensitive to opportunities that will maximize material gains and less sensitive to dependency needs in others. Increasing or decreasing the strength of the evoking stimuli (amount of money offered or amount of dependency shown) should correspondingly alter the impulsive individual's level of cooperative behavior.

CHAPTER 8

Vocational Choice

The previous chapters explored the consequence of differences in the core behaviors of impulsiveness as they were related to interpersonal relations and influence. In the present chapter we examine the consequence of these core behaviors for vocational choice.

Personality has been repeatedly identified as one of several factors influencing the individual's occupational preference and subsequent work adjustment. Given an open labor market, the necessary aptitudes and skills, adequate vocational training opportunities, and the like, Super (1957) has hypothesized that "the occupation preferred by an individual should be one in which the individual expects to be the kind of person he perceives himself as being, to assuume a (work) role which is congenial and compatible with his self-concept" (page 232). If the individual, for instance, sees himself as an active, physically competent person, he should be more attracted to a work role that will allow him to implement these aspects of his self-concept, than to a work role that is inconsistent with his self-concept. Super's approach, although attractive in principle, suffers from an inability to specify the relevant dimensions of work that are likely to attract or repel individuals.

Holland (1966; 1968) has amplified Super's views in a general theory of vocational choice that includes an attempt to describe the dimensions of work relevant to occupational choice behavior. This theory describes six personality types that presumably cover the domain of personality related to vocational choice; six vocational environments are also described that cover the various kinds of work environments that may exist. The general prediction of the theory is that individuals will be most attracted to and most satisfied with vocations (or more precisely, their task demands) that are congruent with the individual's personality type.

Although one may feel a certain arbitrariness underlying Holland's choice of the domains of personality and environments, his descriptions provide a conceptual frame sufficiently specific to undertake empirical studies. My interest in Holland's theory is based on the fact that two of his personality types appear to overlap with the description of the behavior of impulsive and nonimpulsive persons. Consequently, the predictions generated by Holland's theory may also apply to persons varying in impulsiveness. Specifically of interest are what Holland calls the "intellectual" personality type and the "enterprising" personality type. Holland describes the intellectual type by such adjectives as introverted, task-oriented, self-controlled, unsociable, and as functioning best in a vocational environment that is characterized by tasks that require abstract abilities, and in which achievement is usually gradual, requiring persistence, and taking place over long periods of time. Vocations with these task demands are primarily in the physical science and mathematics fields, according to Holland.

Holland describes the enterprising personality by such adjectives as impulsive, energetic, extroverted, materialistically oriented and aggressive. He is seen as functioning best in vocational environments that stress social interactions and persuasive leadership roles. Vocations with these task demands include business, sales, economics, or law.

The reader will recognize that at least at a descriptive level, the behaviors used by Holland to define his two personality types overlap with the behaviors used to define impulsiveness. Hence, one could predict that the vocational preferences of individuals varying in impulsiveness would be similar to the vocational preferences of Holland's intellectual and enterprising personalities. That is, impulsive persons should prefer careers involving social interactions and avoid careers that require attending to the same intellectual problems for a long period of time.

The first evidence supporting these predictions was obtained from a set of correlations between the Impulsiveness Scale and the Strong Vocational Interest Inventory.* Among the incoming University of Delaware freshmen class reported on in Chapter 3, impulsiveness scores correlated $+.30$ and $+.34$ with interest in a sale's managers position and interest in social science work, respectively, and $-.29$ and $-.35$ with interest in careers in the physical sciences and in mathematics. This pattern of correlations indicates

* My thanks to J. Pemberton, Director of the University of Delaware Counseling Center for providing me with these correlations.

that impulsive individuals are attracted to careers that involve interpersonal contacts and that make use of their persuasive talents. Conversely, they are not attracted to science careers which have a reputation for self-discipline and abstract abilities. Clearly, this pattern of vocational interests is consistent with the predictions of Holland. This pattern is also consistent with the previous findings that nonimpulsive persons "shy" away from close interpersonal contacts.

Vocational Choice

COLLEGE FRESHMEN

In addition to test results, another indication of vocational interest is the number of students who actually apply for training in a given vocational area. Fortunately such information on career choice was available from the University of Delaware sample of entering freshmen ($N = 628$), who were tested as reported above. These students enrolled in one of several colleges, according to their vocational aspirations. For our purposes, these enrollments were classified into three groupings, consisting of those who, at the time they entered Delaware, enrolled in either the College of Liberal Arts, the College of Engineering (including liberal arts engineering), or a third group consisting of the College of Business and Economics, the College of Educations, and the Agricultural College (designated Other Colleges).

From what has already been said, we would expect fewer impulsive than

TABLE 26

CURRICULUM ENROLLMENT

	Impulsive (%)	Moderate (%)	Nonimpulsive (%)
High ability[a]			
Liberal Arts	47	34	42
Engineering	32	51	47
Other Colleges	21	15	11
Total N:	103	104	111
Low ability[b]			
Liberal arts	43	43	52
Engineering	14	12	16
Other Colleges	43	45	32
Total N	123	84	103

[a] Chi square = 11.38, df 4, $p < .05$;
[b] Chi square = 4.20, df, 4, p, ns.

nonimpulsive students to enroll in the engineering curriculum at Delaware, since engineering consists of course work in mathematics and the physical sciences. Enrollment data are shown in Table 26, separately for students with above and below median SAT scores (1101 or more vs. 1100 or less).

Whereas the differences in choice of college between impulsive and non-impulsive students were not dramatic, they were in the predicted direction. Among more intelligent students, fewer impulsive than moderate or non-impulsive students enrolled in the engineering curriculum. More impulsive students chose the Other Colleges, which among high-ability students consisted mainly of business or education. Chi-square analysis within each ability grouping revealed that impulsiveness was significantly related to college enrollment among high-ability students ($p < .05$), but not among low-ability students.

UPPER CLASSMEN

The previous study was based upon the vocational choices of students who were just entering college. In the next study we attempted to extend the findings to more advanced students. To this end, a sample of Temple University students in their senior year who majored in either business management ($N = 30$) or mathematics, chemistry, and physics ($N = 30$) were randomly selected from departmental lists of students majoring in these two areas. These students were contacted and asked to take the Impulsiveness Scale as part of a study of vocational interest. There were four refusals. The prediction of this study was that mathematics and science majors would have lower impulsiveness scores than would business management majors.

The average Impulsiveness Score for business management majors was 17.27 and for mathematics and physical science majors it was 13.53 ($F = 7.81$, $df\ 1/58$, $p < .01$). To test for the possible moderating effects of intelligence, a subanalysis was made using only students with combined SAT scores of 1000 or more, a median score for Temple University. For this more intelligent group, the results were intensified. The average impulsiveness score for business majors was 19.31 and for physical science majors it was 12.96 ($F = 12.16$, $df\ 1/34$, $p < .01$). In short, the prediction was supported among more intelligent students. Impulsive students chose what Holland would term an enterprising environment and nonimpulsive students chose an intellectual environment.

Vocational Satisfaction

In the preceding study not all nonimpulsive students chose science as their major and not all impulsive students majored in business management.

Presumably where personality and vocational environment did not mesh, one could expect dissatisfaction with choice of major. That is, the impulsive science major should find that the task demands of his major required more concentration and daily effort than he was prepared to give, whereas the nonimpulsive business major should have found the rather loose organization and practical orientation of business courses not to his liking. Holland (1966, pp. 73–74) cites several studies to support the general notion that a person is likely to remain satisfied with his field of study when his interests and/or personality are congruent with the task demands of his vocation.

To test the above views, the 30 Temple University students majoring in business management and the 30 students majoring in mathematics and the physical sciences each rated on a 5-point scale how satisfied they were with their choice of college major (5 = most satisfied). The product-moment correlation between impulsiveness scores and the ratings of satisfaction made by mathematics and physical science students was $-.67$ (df, 28, $p < .01$). Those impulsive students who chose mathematics or the physical sciences as their major were more dissatisfied with their choice than were non-impulsive students. Among mathematics and physical science majors with SAT scores of 1000 or more, the correlation between satisfaction and impulsiveness rose to $-.88$ ($p < .01$).

The corresponding correlation between the Impulsiveness Scale and ratings of satisfaction with choice of major among business students was $+.01$, providing no support for the prediction of a relation between personality and satisfaction. Subanalysis among business students with SAT scores over 1000 did not appreciably raise this correlation. Only SAT scores correlated with ratings of satisfaction among business students ($r = .64$, $p < .01$), suggesting that intellectual ability was an important determinant of vocational satisfaction among this group. SAT scores did not correlate significantly with satisfaction among mathematics and physical science majors, although the correlation was still positive ($r = .21$).

Actually intellectual ability has influenced career choice in a major fashion in the two samples studied, and its influence deserves some comment. In the University of Delaware sample, engineering students were almost completely drawn from among more intelligent students. At Temple University, 82% of the mathematics and physical science majors had SAT scores over 1000, as compared to 42% of the business majors. It is plain that cognitive ability had more of an influence on career choice than personality, at least in terms of the occupational fields reported on here. Apparently, a necessary condition for the choice of the physical sciences as a career seems to be a modestly high level of intelligence. Once this condition is satisfied, factors such as impulsiveness begin to exert their influence. Within the context of this explanation, the lack of correlation between SAT scores and satisfaction with choice of major among mathematics and physical science majors may be a result of the restricted range of their SAT scores. In psychological terms, it may be that most mathematics and physical science majors had sufficient ability to master their work, and hence satisfactions were determined by other personal factors, such as impulsiveness.

Changes in Major Area of Vocational Choice

An indirect measure of satisfaction with vocational choice may be had by examining the numbers of persons who changed their major during the course of their college careers. Stability of career choice was available for the University of Delaware sample through the completion of their sophomore year. In line with the arguments presented thus far, it could be expected that more impulsive than nonimpulsive students would transfer from engineering to one of the other colleges. Table 27 shows the proportions of students originally enrolled in each of the three colleges who elected to transfer during their first two years. In addition, Table 27 shows the proportion of originally enrolled students who dropped out of Delaware. These findings are only given for those students with above median SAT scores. There were too few engineering students in the below-median group to make comparisons meaningful.

Although impulsive students had the highest rate of attrition from engineering, it can be seen that their attrition rate from all colleges was rather high. Furthermore, nonimpulsive students also had a high attrition

TABLE 27

STUDENTS CHANGING COLLEGES OR DROPPING OUT OF DELAWARE
FOR ACADEMIC REASONS

	Impulsive (N = 103)			Moderate (N = 104)			Nonimpulsive (N = 111)		
	Transferred %	Drop-out %	Total sample %	Transferred %	Drop-out %	Total sample %	Transferred %	Drop-out %	Total sample %
Liberal Arts	13	27	40	7	23	30	0	9	9
Engineering	28	30	58	13	20	33	19	21	40
Other Colleges	9	23	32	19	31	50	8	8	16
Adjusted totals	16	28	43	12	23	35	10	14	24

rate from engineering, although not as high as impulsive students. This would suggest that personality per se accounted for only a part of the attrition from engineering. Course difficulty was presumably the major factor. In any case the data presented in Table 27 do not support the prediction that impulsiveness would be more strongly related to attrition among engineering students than among students in the other two colleges.

As a final point, it can be seen that the number of impulsive students dropping out of Delaware after two years enrollment was about double that of nonimpulsive students (28% versus 14%). This finding is consistent with the data on achievement presented in Chapter 2.

Vocational Choice and Achievement

In addition to attraction to and satisfaction with a vocational role, the rationale given in the introduction to this chapter implies that impulsive students should underachieve in the study of physical science, in comparison with their studies of other vocational areas. This is because the task demands of the natural sciences, especially in the early stages of study should be inconsistent with the restless behaviors of the impulsive student. Beginning physical science courses generally require constant class attendance and home study, including the solving of assigned problems, in order to follow the developing logic of the courses. It is generally agreed that once a student falls behind in his science assignments, it becomes difficult for him to catch up. This is because each unit of course work presupposes understanding of past work. Thus a haphazard pattern of classroom attendance and home study will leave the student poorly prepared for final examinations. The same pattern of day-to-day diligence seems less necessary, however, for courses in the social sciences and humanities. The interdependence between various ideas presented in these courses is often rather slight. As a result, students are frequently able to make up missed assignments through prodigious stints of reading and writing immediately prior to final examinations.

The first evidence of differential achievement has been noted in Table 27, in terms of the numbers of Delaware students who were dropped from each of the three colleges. As could be seen, this evidence was negative. Impulsive students dropped out at an equally high level from all three college groupings, rather than showing the predicted highest failure rate in the Engineering College grouping.

The next evidence of differential achievement was in terms of the grades of 216 Temple University freshmen in introductory courses in psychology and mathematics. Their achievement in these two courses was analyzed by means of 3×3 factorial design, with three levels of impulsiveness (Impulsive-

ness Index) and three levels of intellectual ability as measured by SAT
scores (940 or less; 941–1060; 1061 or more) constituting the independent
variables. Final grades in both courses, expressed on a 0 (= F) to 4 (= A)
scale, were entered as the dependent measures.

The results of the analyses of variance (Table 28) indicated that impulsiveness was not significantly related to final grades in psychology, but was
significantly related to mathematics grades ($p < .05$).

TABLE 28

SUMMARY OF ANALYSIS OF VARIANCE: MATHEMATICS AND INTRODUCTORY PSYCHOLOGY

Source	Mathematics			Psychology		
	df	MS	F	df	MS	F
Impulsiveness	2	3.77	3.12[a]	2	1.35	1.32
Intellectual ability	2	1.46	1.20	2	12.15	11.89[b]
Interaction	4	2.15	1.77	4	.08	1
Error	207	1.21		207	1.02	

[a] $p < .05$
[b] $p < .01$

Table 28 shows that impulsive students earned lower mathematics grades
than moderate or nonimpulsive students. Furthermore, the trend appears to
be that as intellectual ability increased, the relation between impulsiveness
and mathematics grades also increased. Since these findings were consistent
with past findings on the moderating influence of ability, it was decided to
compute separate F tests between mathematics grades and impulsiveness
within each ability level. These separate tests found that the relation between
impulsiveness and mathematics grades was only significant among students
who were in the top third of intellectual ability ($p < .01$). The differences in

TABLE 29

AVERAGE MATHEMATICS GRADE

Intellectual ability	Impulsive		Moderate		Nonimpulsive	
	X̄	N	X̄	N	X̄	N
High third	1.46	24	1.80	15	2.55	20
Middle third	1.93	28	2.05	21	2.27	22
Low third	1.77	26	1.93	29	1.74	31

grades between impulsive, moderates and nonimpulsive students was not significant among those students in the middle or bottom thirds of intellectual ability.

The achievement of impulsive students in science and non-science courses could also be examined among the 30 business management and the 30 mathematics and physical science majors discussed earlier in this chapter. In this instance, scores on the Impulsiveness Scale were correlated with students grade-point averages for the term as a means of examining this relationship. For mathematics and physical science majors the correlation between impulsiveness and grades was −.13, and for business management majors, the correlation was +.11. Among students with SAT scores of 1000 or more, the correlations remained insignificant. These findings then do not support the differential achievement hypothesis.

A final study providing evidence on the relation between impulsiveness and science grades was obtained from the 2-year cumulative grades of the University of Delaware students who did not drop out of school. In this instance it was expected that the largest differential in cumulative grade-point average between impulsive and nonimpulsive students should occur among those majoring in engineering. Table 30 shows these grades for above the median SAT students. The last column in Table 29 gives the results of an analysis of variance within each college grouping.

TABLE 30

CUMULATIVE 2-YEAR GRADE-POINT INDEX FOR NON-DROPS AT DELAWARE
(High Ability Students)

College groupings	Impulsive		Moderates		Nonimpulsive		
	$\bar{X}$	N	$\bar{X}$	N	$\bar{X}$	N	F
Liberal Arts	2.44	35	2.42	26	2.68	43	3.42[a]
Engineering	2.34	23	2.48	43	2.73	41	6.42[b]
Other colleges	2.35	17	2.62	11	2.52	11	1.23 ns

[a] $p < .05$
[b] $p < .01$

The strongest relation between impulsiveness and grades occurred in the engineering college, although a significant relation was also obtained in the Liberal Arts college. We may view these findings as modestly supporting the idea of differential achievement, in that impulsive students had the lowest grades in engineering and nonimpulsive students had the highest grades.

Summary

The findings were consistent with the view that impulsive and restless persons would be less attracted to vocations that required day-to-day persistence and study, as represented by courses in the physical sciences and mathematics. At a more general level, the findings were also supportive of the view proposed by Super and Holland that people search for environments and vocations that permit them to satisfy and express their personalities. At both Temple and Delaware, nonimpulsive students sought what Holland would term an intellectual or scientific environment, whereas impulsive students were more attracted to business careers. The findings further revealed that impulsive students who entered the field of science did not find it to their liking. Less satisfaction was expressed by impulsive than by nonimpulsive students over their choice of science as an academic major. Furthermore, nonimpulsive students appeared to achieve better grades and impulsive students somewhat poorer grades in the sciences than in the nonsciences. However, the data supporting this last assertion were weak. In only one study (introductory psychology versus introductory mathematics) were the differences clear-cut, suggesting that additional studies are needed to verify this point.

There also appears to be a need for long-term follow-up studies of the relation between vocational choice and personality beyond the undergraduate level. Does the impulsive business major actually enter a business career more frequently than the nonimpulsive business major? If so, what type of businessman does he make? Presumably the impulsive businessman should be less constrained by standards and more ready to take advantage of opportunities with less thought as to the welfare of competitors. One also wonders whether graduate school applications for training in the physical sciences are received mainly from nonimpulsive students. Certainly these findings fit the stereotype of the scientist as serious and introverted, patiently working for long years in his laboratory. Yet in a sense they fit too neatly. One has but to read *The Double Helix,* by Watson to understand that the stereotype of the introspective scientist is considerably overdrawn. Advances in science are frequently made by persons who are willing to challenge the basic dogmas that clutter any area of research and who are willing to make intuitive and often wildly illogical inferences concerning the nature of reality. I would guess that this kind of contribution is less likely to be made by nonimpulsive researchers. In a different context Barron (1963) has described the difficulties of truly creative graduate students in satisfying the formal requirements of their graduate school. Many of the behaviors that Barron ascribes to these creative graduate students may be also discerned among students described here as impulsive. If one can coordinate these two lines of personality description, it would suggest that training in the natural sciences may be repelling many individuals who have the potential for making important contributions.

CHAPTER 9

Prevention of Underachievement

It was pointed out in Chapter 2 that psychological research has achieved modest success in developing tests capable of identifying students who are likely to underachieve. A next step in research might well be to use the information provided by tests to devise treatments to reduce underachievement. In part, this procedure is already being followed in counseling and guidance programs, where psychological tests are used by counselors when planning how to help their clients. McClelland and Winter's (1969) attempts to teach the achievement motive to persons with low need-achievement scores also have this goal in mind. On the other hand, this procedure is used infrequently in business and educational institutions. In these institutions, tests are used mainly to identify and reject applicants likely to fail.

The findings reported in Chapters 3 and 8 indicated that one could predict underachievement among bright students in terms of impulsiveness test scores. Hence, the information provided by the tests could be used to institute a program of preventative treatment. This chapter presents the results of a study by the author in collaboration with Jerome Resnick that attempted to elevate the academic performance of impulsive university students, prior to their actual experience of underachievement. As Spielberger, Denny, and Weitz (1962) have noted, initiation of treatment after the student has gotten into academic difficulty has not proven very effective for elevating performance.

Rationale for the Study

Let us first review the evidence presented in the previous chapters as to why bright impulsive students underachieve. Clearly, lack of ability is not the reason. We have shown that as intellectual level increased, so too did the failure rate among impulsive persons. In order to understand the reasons for failure, we must consider the behaviors and attitudes that define the construct of impulsiveness, as these have been explored in the previous chapters. The behaviors that seem most clearly related to underachievement were those involved in restlessness and sensation seeking. These behaviors were presumed to be manifested in poor study habits, inattention in class, and sporadic class attendance. Thus, therapeutic procedures devised for this group should aim at encouraging more systematic study and attention to school work. The question, of course, is how to achieve this aim. Before presenting our solution to this question, it is necessary to review other research findings that influenced our thinking. These additional findings centered around impulsive students' responses to interpersonal influence and failure situations.

The first consideration involves the finding that impulsive students do not experience much embarrassment, shame, or anxiety in situations that have the potential for evoking such negative feelings. Because of this, we felt that impulsive persons would be less likely to experience genuine psychological distress over academic underachievement. In turn, this lack of psychic distress might inhibit the development of motivation to improve performance or to seek out professional advice as to how to improve. Furthermore, even if impulsive persons were somehow induced to seek guidance from a counselor, the evidence from the present research, as well as evidence from clinical populations (Cairns, 1961; Hetherington and Klinger, 1964; Johns and Quay, 1962; Sarbin, Allen and Rutherford, 1965) suggests a generalized resistance among impulsive persons to the advice and counsel of others.

Since impulsive individuals are less likely to be motivated by psychic distress, or social rewards resulting from the expectation of successful task completion, or by the advice of friends and counselors, the question arises as to whether any class of incentives exists which does have enough reinforcing strength to motivate persons into therapy designed to help improve their performance. The answer arrived at is perhaps obvious, from what has already been said. We chose to use money as the incentive to motivate impulsive students into treatment; that is, we decided to pay impulsive students what amounted to a salary for behaving in ways designed to elevate their academic performance.

Two treatment conditions were designed for this study. In the first, impulsive and nonimpulsive students were paid a weekly salary, contingent upon their demonstrating that they had completed their previous week's assignment in a college introductory mathematics course. Mathematics was chosen because of the findings, discussed in Chapter 8, that this area of study presented the greatest difficulties to impulsive students. It was predicted that impulsive students would study their mathematics assignments in order to receive the weekly payments. We hoped that this increased weekly effort would result in higher grades at the end of the semester.

The second treatment-condition consisted of paying impulsive and nonimpulsive students to attend group counseling each week. This form of treatment is the major current method used to elevate the performance of underachieving students. It was our expectation that impulsive students would not benefit from counseling, for reasons stated above.

Procedure

The students were entering Temple University freshmen with total SAT scores of 1,000 or more. They were selected from low income families as determined by the Temple University financial office on the basis of application filed for financial aid, or by a review of the parent's occupation. The reason for restricting the sample by economic level was to ensure that the financial incentive offered would be attractive to the participants. In retrospect, it appears that this restriction was unnecessarily severe. Informal conversations with students has subsequently revealed that the amount of money offered ($10/week) would have been a valuable source of income to practically all students.

The selection of students occurred in two stages. The first stage sought to identify bright impulsive students before they entered the university. To this end, prior to the beginning of the fall semester, incoming freshmen identified as being of low income level were contacted by letter and asked to visit the university to complete a set of questionnaires relating to their background and interests. They were told that they would also be contacted at the end of the semester to obtain information on their experiences at the university. Included in the questionnaires were the two impulsiveness scales. Of the 226 students contacted, 201 were tested. The 25 remaining students lived too far from the university to visit before the semester began, or simply did not respond to the letter inviting them to visit.

Following the initial testing, a sample of the above students, classified as being impulsive or not on the basis of the Impulsiveness Index, were invited by letter to participate in an experimental scholarship program designed to help them defray weekly living expenses. Weekly payments of

$10 were offered. Only one student (non-impulsive) refused to participate, stating he did not need the money. Groups of 16 impulsive and 16 non-impulsive impulsive were randomly assigned to each of the four conditions. The conditions were: (1) Paid-Math; (2) Paid-counseling; (3) Paid-control; (4) No-pay control. Students in the No-pay control were not contacted beyond the initial letter asking them to complete the questionnaires. The program and payments were started at the beginning of the second week of the first semester. Since the university had just adopted a 13-week semester period, payments were made for 12 weeks, for a maximum possible total of $120 per student.

PAID-MATH CONDITION

Students assigned to this condition were told that in order to receive their $10 week scholarship payment, they would have to maintain a satisfactory level in their mathematics course. Evidence that they were maintaining this level would be demonstrated by their passing a weekly quiz. The students were enrolled in either a basic course in finite mathematics or a more advanced course in calculus.

The quizzes were prepared by a member of the Mathematics Department and followed the teaching syllabus for each course. Each quiz consisted of 10 to 15 multiple-choice questions. Testing time ranged from 15 to 30 minutes depending upon the student. The relevance of the quizzes to the course content was high, as estimated by correlations with final mathematics grades. Scores on the quizzes summed over the first six weeks correlated .63 ($p < .01$) with final mathematics grade and .72 ($p < .01$) when summed over the entire 12 weeks.

The tests were administered each Monday by an assistant, in a setting apart from the regular classroom. They were graded immediately, and if the student passed he was paid $10 on the spot. Mathematics instructors were not aware of this program on any systematic basis, although individual students may have asked their instructors about the program. For the first 3 weeks, all students were given passing grades. After this time, a passing grade of between 50% to 60% was set. One impulsive student was lost halfway through the semester when, after finding that he could not pass the quizzes, he resigned from the study. A second impulsive student withdrew from the university after 6 weeks to join the army. Both of these students' grades were included in the data anaylsis. It should be noted that the inclusion of these two students' failing grades is a conservative procedure that reduced the possibility of finding treatment effects. It is also important to note that no attempt was made to provide students with additional tutoring at the time of the weekly quizzes. Feedback was limited to telling students which items they had answered incorrectly.

PAID COUNSELING

Students met once a week in groups of six to nine. There were two counselors assigned to each group. Each session lasted for approximately 45 minutes. The students were paid $10/week conditional upon their having attended that week's meeting. Of the 32 students in this condition, 25 attended all 12 meetings, five students missed one meeting, and one student missed two meetings. No student missed more than this number of meetings except for one impulsive student who dropped out of school halfway through the semester. This student's grades were included in the data analysis. We also inadvertently included one impulsive student attending the university high school. This student was dropped from the analysis.

The group discussions were open-ended, with the general focus on academic adjustment and vocational goals. There was also some discussion of personal adjustment. A fair amount of discussion centered on university requirements or university indifference to the student. Counselors reported that the students were not particularly motivated to attend these sessions. Most of the students stated that they did not have any problems; their attendance being merely to receive the $10. The majority of counselors felt that the lack of motivation among the students precluded the establishment of a genuine counseling situation.

The counselors were members of the university counseling center and all had graduate degrees and extensive previous experience in counseling and clinical work with students. Because of class scheduling difficulties, no attempt was made to arrange groups in terms of impulsiveness. Rather groups were scheduled solely in terms of there being enough students with a common free period.

PAID CONTROL

This group merely came in once a week to collect their scholarship payment. We inadvertently included one impulsive and two nonimpulsive music majors in this group. Since these three students took a completely different set of courses, they were not included in the data analysis.

NO-PAY CONTROL

This group was contacted at the end of the semester to fill out a set of postsemester questionnaires. Otherwise the group had no contact with the experiment. One impulsive student dropped out of the university prior to completing the semester. His grades were included in the data analysis.

Questionnaires

At the beginning of the semester all students were asked how much money they expected to actually have for weekly living expenses. They were also asked how satisfied they were with this estimated amount. Their answers to these questions, which were given in detail in Chapter 4, indicated that impulsive students were more dissatisfied than nonimpulsive students with the amount of spending money they had available during the semester.

Another questionnaire asked students to describe themselves on a set of nine bipolar rating scales containing such items as dependable–undependable; dislikes school–likes school. Of interest was the finding that impulsive students, when compared to nonimpulsive students, described themselves as less dependable ($p < .05$); as having poorer study habits ($p < .08$); and as disliking school ($p < .01$). These findings are consistent with our original descriptions of impulsive individuals. At the end of the semester, students again completed the bipolar scales and answered questions concerning their attitudes toward the experiments and toward the university.

Criteria of Academic Performance

Mathematics final grade expressed on a 0–4 scale ($F = 0$ and $A = 4$) was the first criterion used. In addition the mathematics grade was dichotomized at the median of the grade distribution into those who received a B or better and those who received a C or less. Dropouts were assigned a grade of F.

Overall Final grade expressed on a 0–4 scale ($A = 4$) was the second criterion used. In addition, the overall final grade was dichotomized at the median of the grade distribution into those who received a 2.51 or better (C+) and those who received 2.50 or less. Dropouts from the university were assigned a grade of .75.

Analysis

Analysis of variance was used to evaluate the influence of the treatment conditions upon the grades. The dichotomized grades were analyzed through chi square. Since our major predictions concerned impulsive students, separate statistics comparisions between treatment conditions and the control condition were made at each level of impulsiveness.

Our prior research had found strongest results for impulsiveness among Temple students with upper third SAT scores of 1060 or more (see Chapter 8). The present study used a median cut-off scores on the SAT of 1000 or more. Since it would found that the higher the intellectual level of students, the stronger the relations between impulsiveness and behavior, a second set of analyses were carried out using only students with SAT scores of 1060 or more. In this second analysis 37 students were eliminated.

For the total sample there were no differences in SAT scores between the experimental conditions or between impulsive and nonimpulsive students ($F < 1$). However for the subsample of students with SAT scores of 1060 or more, impulsive students in the Paid-math condition had higher SAT scores than impulsive students in the control conditions. This difference in SAT scores presented no problem in analyzing mathematics grades, since SAT scores correlated $+.05$ with these grades. However, SAT scores were correlated with final semester grades ($r = .28$) among impulsive students. Accordingly, analysis of covariance was used in the final grade analysis as a means of equating groups on SAT score. In the chi-square analysis, samples were matched for SAT scores when the overall chi squares were statistically significant. Chi square was then recomputed on these matched students.

Results

CONTROL ANALYSIS

A comparison of the Paid-control group to the Unpaid-control group with respect to mathematics grades and to final semester grades revealed no differences in performance between these groups ($p < .50$). Whatever benefits providing students with a weekly allowance may have, these benefits did not relate to academic performance. In the subsequent analyses, the Paid and Unpaid control groups were merged to provide a more stable baseline for estimating the effects of the Paid-math and Paid-counseling conditions.

The next analysis compared the grades of impulsive students to non-impulsive students in the combined control condition. Impulsive students in the combined control condition had a final grade-point average of 2.01 and nonimpulsive students had a final grade-point average of 2.68. By F test, this difference in overall achievement was significant beyond the .01 level ($F = 17.62$, df $1/59$, p, ns). Only 13% of the impulsive students had final grades above the median of 2.51, while 63% of the nonimpulsive students had above median grades. These findings support our original contention that tests of impulsiveness could identify in advance students likely to underachieve.

Mathematics Grades

Given that impulsive students did underachieve, we next considered the question of whether the experimental manipulations were effective in elevating their grades? The results were nonsignificant when mathematics grades were considered alone. Table 31 shows these findings. Despite the fact that the mathematics grades in the Paid-math condition were elevated in the predicted direction, they were not significantly higher than those in the control conditions. The Paid-counseling condition also did not differ significantly from the control condition.

TABLE 31

AVERAGE MATHEMATICS GRADES

	Average mathematics grade						% Above median mathematics grade (B or better)		
	Paid-math		Paid-counsel		Control		Paid-math	Paid-counsel	Control
	$\bar{X}$	N	$\bar{X}$	N	$\bar{X}$	N			
Impulsive	2.25	(16)	2.47	(15)	1.97	(31)	50%	53%	35%
Nonimpulsive	2.88	(16)	2.80	(16)	2.57	(30)	75%	60%	53%

Whereas the results for all students were not significant, the subanalysis among students with SAT scores of 1060 or more was significant (see Table 32). Both the analysis of variance and the chi-square analysis found that impulsive and nonimpulsive students in the Paid-math condition had significantly higher mathematics grades than students in the control conditions ($F = 4.46$, $df\ 1/60$, $p < .05$; chi square $= 6.19$, $p < .02$). Mathematics grades in the Paid-counseling condition did not differ significantly from the control condition.

TABLE 32

FINAL MATHEMATICS GRADES AMONG STUDENTS WITH SAT SCORES OF 1060 OR MORE

	Average mathematics grade						% Above median mathematics grade (B or better)		
	Paid-math		Paid-counsel		Control		Paid-math	Paid-counsel	Control
	$\bar{X}$	N	$\bar{X}$	N	$\bar{X}$	N			
Impulsive	3.00	10	2.46	11	2.37	19	80%	54%	46%
Nonimpulsive	3.31	13	3.09	12	2.64	22	85%	73%	54%

FINAL SEMESTER GRADES

As shown in Table 33 the final grades of nonimpulsive students were not increased by either treatment condition. However the final grades of impulsive students were significantly elevated by the Paid-counseling condition ($F = 5.40$, df 1/44, $p < .05$; $X^2 = 11.06$, $p < .01$). The Paid-math condition also elevated impulsive students grades. However the analysis of variance comparing the Paid-math and control condition was not statistically significant, although the chi-square comparison of the same data was significant ($X^2 = 5.60$, $p < .05$).

TABLE 33

AVERAGE SEMESTER GRADE FOR ALL STUDENTS

	Average semester grade[a]			% Above median semester grade (2.51 or better)		
	Paid-math $\bar{X}$	Paid-counsel $\bar{X}$	Control $\bar{X}$	Paid-math	Paid-counsel	Control
Impulsive	2.22	2.49	2.01	44%	60%	13%
Nonimpulsive	2.66	2.62	2.68	69%	62%	63%

[a] See Table 31 for values of N.

The final semester grades of students with SAT scores of 1060 or more are given in Table 34. Here again it can be seen that the experimental treatments had little influence upon the grades of nonimpulsive students. However, among the more intelligent impulsive students, both the Paid-math condition and the Paid-counseling condition significantly elevated final grades. This can be seen most clearly in terms of the numbers of impulsive students in each condition who exceeded the median final grade of 2.51.

TABLE 34

OVERALL SEMESTER GRADES AMONG STUDENTS WITH SAT SCORES OF 1060 OR MORE

	Average semester grades[a]			% Above median semester grade (2.51 or better)		
	Paid-math $\bar{X}$	Paid-counsel $\bar{X}$	Control $\bar{X}$	Paid-math	Paid-counsel	Control
Impulsive	2.54	2.50	2.07	70%	64%	16%
Nonimpulsive	2.79	2.81	2.66	77%	75%	64%

[a] See Table 32 for values of N.

The numbers exceeding this median in both the Paid-math and the Paid-counseling conditions were significantly higher than in the control condition ($p < .05$ by chi-square test, controling for SAT scores). The parallel findings using analyses of co-variance revealed that grades in both the Paid-math and the Paid-counseling conditions exceeded the control condition beyond the .10 level of confidence.

SUBANALYSIS OF FINAL GRADES

The higher final grades of impulsive students in the Paid-math condition could be due to the specific contribution of their higher mathematics grades or to the general elevation of their course grades. To investigate these alternatives, a new final grade was computed for each student which excluded the mathematics grade. Table 35 shows this corrected final grade. It can be seen that impulsive students' grades in the Paid-math condition remained elevated even after the contribution of mathematics has been removed. Apparently, paying bright impulsive students to study mathematics influenced their academic performance in their other courses as well.

TABLE 35

FINAL SEMESTER GRADES MINUS MATHEMATICS GRADES OF STUDENTS WITH SAT SCORES OF 1060 OR HIGHER

	Corrected semester grade[a]			% Above median corrected grade (2.50 or better)		
	Paid-math $\bar{X}$	Paid-counsel $\bar{X}$	Control $\bar{X}$	Paid-math	Paid-counsel	Control
Impulsive	2.43	2.48	1.92	60%	54%	16%
Nonimpulsive	2.63	2.75	2.65	61%	83%	59%

[a] See Table 32 for values of N.

SECOND SEMESTER GRADES

It was of interest to determine whether the grades of impulsive students during the second semester were in any way influenced by the experimental treatments. In this second semester, of course, the scholarship payments and associated treatment conditions had ceased. The participants had resumed their regular status as students and were no longer singled out for any kind of special attention. Table 36 gives the second semester grades of students who still remained at Temple. Excluded from this analysis were 10 impulsive students (16% of the total) and three nonimpulsive students (5%) who were dropped for academic reasons before the beginning of the second semester.

An additional two nonimpulsive students who transferred to other universities with acceptable grade point averages during their first semester (2.8 and 3.5) were also excluded.

TABLE 36

SECOND SEMESTER GRADE-POINT AVERAGES

	Paid-math		Paid-counsel		Control	
	$\bar{X}$	N	$\bar{X}$	N	$\bar{X}$	N
Impulsive	2.14	12	2.48	13	2.04	27
Nonimpulsive	2.50	16	2.68	14	2.50	27

It is clear from Table 36 that the Paid-counseling condition continued to positively influence the grades of impulsive students. Differences in grades between the Paid-counseling and Control condition among impulsive students was significant beyond the .05 level ($F = 4.96$, $df 1/38$). None of the remaining comparisons reached statistically significant levels, either among all students or among those with SAT's above 1060.

Attitudes

The scholarship payments had no significant influence upon paid students attitudes toward the university when compared to the views of the nonpaid controls. This was true among all students and among students with SAT scores of 1060 or more. However, there was a trend for impulsive students to express greater dissatisfaction with the amount of interest the university took in its students ($p < .05$). In terms of self-ratings, or changes in self-ratings, from the beginning to the end of the semester, once again there were no significant changes that could be attributed to the experimental treatments. We can conclude that although the two treatment methods were able to significantly influence the actual behavior of impulsive students, they were not influential in changing their attitudes, at least in terms of any of the measures used here.

Discussion

The findings presented in this chapter demonstrated the promise of using diagnostic tests to aid in the prevention of underachievement. Given that one could identify the potential underachiever, it has been argued here that the next step should be to devise therapeutic procedures to treat the specific causes of underachievement, as revealed by the tests. For instance, many people underachieve, not because they are impulsive, but rather because they are anxious. For these people the treatment of choice might involve tranquilizing drugs, counseling, or relaxation training. Others underachieve because of low intelligence *viz* the demands of the tasks. For these persons the treatment might involve reducing the range and amount of cognitive material that they are required to master at any point in time. Instead of 15 to 18 credit hours each semester, for instance, low-intelligence university students might only take 3 to 9 credit hours as a full-time course load.

In the present instance, underachievement among impulsive students was attributed to a restless, sensation-seeking style of life, which we assumed interfered with day-to-day diligence in academic matters. The Paid-math condition was devised in an attempt to disrupt this cycle by offering impulsive students money as an incentive to study.

The Paid-math condition was found to be partially effective in that only the grades of more intelligent impulsive students were improved. Furthermore the influence of this condition did not persist beyond the semester in which payments were in force. However, we should note that among more intelligent students, the mathematics grade (though not overall grades) of nonimpulsive students were also elevated, suggesting some generality for this procedure. Paying students with average intelligence to study mathematics on the other hand was not effective. A possible explanation for this lack of effectiveness was that we made no attempt to tutor students by briefly explaining their errors on the weekly math quizzes. To the extent that a student had real difficulties in understanding the mathematics course, the Paid-math condition would not have been too much help. Its focus was on improving study habits, rather than improving comprehension. One direction for further research would be to ascertain the usefulness of brief tutoring of students on the quiz items they answered incorrectly.

It was also found that paying impulsive students to attend weekly group counseling improved their academic performance. Furthermore, the influence of counseling persisted beyond the counseling period. To say the least, this finding was not expected. Both the present writer's studies and studies in the clinical literature reveal the difficulties associated with trying to change the behavior of persons with impulsive character structures. As was stated in the introduction to this chapter, the problems of influencing change center around two areas, without any clear distinction between them. The first problem is concerned with the unwillingness of impulsive individuals to enter therapy, because they do not experience strong or lasting states of psychological discomfort. It is generally accepted that these distressful affective states are the basic reasons for seeking therapeutic help.

This problem was dealt with here by substituting money for distress as an incentive for remaining in therapy.

The second problem emphasized in the literature is the difficulty of changing behavior among impulsive individuals, once they are in therapy. This difficulty has often been attributed to aversive properties attached to close interpersonal relationships.

It is suggested that in the present study, the continual association of money with the counseling situation may have served to reduce the aversiveness of that situation, so new behaviors could be learned.

The use of money as an incentive to guide students in the various treatment conditions deserves further comment. Psychologists generally tend to de-emphasize money as a source of motivation in our society. Explanations of behavior favor the fulfillment of non-economic kinds of needs. Yet even a cursory examination of our society reveals how behavior is influenced by attempts to satisfy economic goals. In the present study only one non-impulsive student refused to participate in the study. Furthermore, students voluntarily attended counseling for 12 weeks—a period of time far beyond that found in most studies of counseling. This refusal and voluntary attendance rate is impressive when compared to other studies that have attempted to enlist persons for counseling who were not experiencing adjustment problems at the time of recruitment. For instance, Spielberger, Denny and Weitz (1962) invited 112 incoming freshmen who had high scores on the Taylor Manifest Anxiety Scale to participate in voluntary group counseling; 56 (50%) refused. Of those who participated, only 34% attended counseling with any great frequency. Ewing and Gilbert (1967) invited 118 high-aptitude freshmen to participate in four counseling sessions; 28 (24%) refused. The mean number of counseling sessions attended was 3.26. Ewing and Gilbert's study is also of interest because of their finding that the non-volunteer most consistently underachieved in grades. Spielberger, Denny and Weitz also found that students who quit counseling had the lowest grades. Hence, the very persons who would most benefit from counseling were those who refused to participate or dropped out.

Not infrequently the objection raised to the use of money for desired performance is that it would serve primarily to reinforce and consolidate the essential characterological immaturity of subjects. It is feared that tangible reinforcements would cause the person to become dependent on them, so that he would not work unless material reinforcements were supplied. Anderson (1967) found no evidence for this view in a recent review of this question. Schwitzgebel (1969) has examined the arguments against the use of material reinforcements and concludes that the fears raised over their use are groundless. The present study also found no evidence that would counterindicate the use of this form of incentives. Indeed compared to the usual lump-sum forms of scholarship payments which demand no or little contingent effort from the recipient, this use of money appears to have much to recommend it.

Summary

A final issue that should be examined concerns the process through which the grades of impulsive students in both treatment conditions were improved. It was clear from the comments of the counselors that the majority of students only participated to receive the money. Many weeks were spent merely trying to decide what to talk about. In the counselors' opinions a genuine therapeutic relationship was not established. Yet despite these beliefs, grades of impulsive students were raised. Why? Similarly, despite the fact that we paid bright impulsive students only to study mathematics, grades in their remaining courses were also elevated. Again, we ask why? A tentative explanation is that in comparison to the control condition, both treatment conditions forced impulsive students to pay attention to their school progress on a continuing basis. School requirements were the topic of discussion in the counseling sessions. Various course requirements were continually mentioned, even if with some contempt and anger. Math assignments had to be dealt with if the weekly quizzes were to be passed. In the control condition, impulsive students could put off these kinds of consideration. It was not necessary to concern oneself with assignments, except perhaps to decide to put off some assignments until next week, or until before examination time. Perhaps the major contribution of both treatments resided in restructuring the attention of impulsive students to the necessity of not falling too far behind in their studies.

CHAPTER 10

Recapitulation and Some Further Questions

The previous nine chapters discussed detection of the influence of impulsiveness in a wide range of adolescent experiences, ranging from friendship relations to vocational choice. One of the contributions of this book resides, I believe, in showing the pervasiveness of this construct. Of course other investigators have noted similar findings to those in the present volume, but covering a narrower range of experiences. Thus, Zuckerman and his co-workers (1965; 1968) have focused upon variations in sensation-seeking behavior, as measured by his sensation-seeking scale. Christie and Geist (1970) have used the Machiavellianism Scale to study individual differences in exploitive or manipulative behavior, while Gough has used the Socialization Scale to study individual differences in achievement and social adjustment (1965). It appears that each of these investigators has concentrated upon only one part of the proverbial elephant. Eysenck (1957; 1964) is perhaps the major exception to this tendency to focus narrowly. Here, for example, are his descriptions of the behavior of the extrovert and the introvert, as these behaviors are affected by variations in self-control.

> The typical extrovert is sociable, likes parties, has many friends, needs to have people to talk to, and does not like reading or studying by himself. He craves excitement, takes chances, acts on the spur of the moment, and is generally an impulsive person. He is fond of practical jokes, always has a ready answer, and generally likes change; he is carefree, easygoing, opti-

mistic, and likes to laugh and be merry. He prefers to keep moving and doing things, tends to be aggressive and loses his temper quickly; his feelings are not kept under tight control and he is not always a reliable person."

"The typical introvert is a quiet, retiring sort of person, introspective, fond of books rather than people, he is reserved and reticent, except for intimate friends. He tends to plan ahead, looks before he leaps, and distrusts the impulse of the moment. He does not like excitement, takes matters of everyday life with proper seriousness, and likes a well-ordered mode of life. He keeps his feelings under close control, seldom behaves in an aggressive manner, and does not lose his temper easily. He is reliable, somewhat pessimistic, and places great value on ethical standards. (page 36)

In addition to illustrating the broad range of social behaviors influenced by variations in self-control, Eysenck's descriptions raise an issue that we have only briefly mentioned. This issue concerns the nature of the inter-relationship between various sources of control and restraint. Implicit in Eysenck's description is the assumption that the behaviors differentiating the introvert from the extrovert are bipolar and cluster together to form a personality dimension of a fundamental kind. A similar assumption has been made in this volume. Persons who tend to resist social influence are believed to be less reactive to anxiety-provoking stimuli, in greater need of excitement and social stimulation, more exploitive, and less concerned with conventional social norms. On the contrary, those who are open to social influence from others are believed to be more reactive to anxiety-provoking situations, have less need for excitement, and so on.

It is not necessary, however, to assume that these behaviors cluster together in the above manner. Several personality theorists (Sullivan, Grant, and Grant, 1957; Loevinger, 1966) have stated that the relationship between these various restraining behaviors is mediated by the individual's stage of development. Loevinger, for example, believes that ego development proceeds in stagelike progressions and that only within a given stage of development can one make statements concerning how these restraining behaviors relate to each other. Thus, persons fixated at what Loevinger calls an impulse-ridden stage of development may be expected to show poor impulse control and to be highly exploitive of others. At the next highest stage of development (opportunistic) Loevinger believes that the relation between impulse control and exploitation would be nil or slightly negative, since the individual has greater control over his impulses at this stage, but still exploits others.

The research presented in this book does not provide evidence on these conflicting views, since different subjects were used for most of the studies. As a result the interrelations between the various dependent measures could not be determined. We have no way of knowing, for instance, whether the person who stated that he experienced anxiety on the Fear Questionnaire would have been influenced by his friend's judgments in the autokinetic study. To the extent that our tests of impulsiveness were heterogeneous, these tests could be related to several dimensions of behavior that were, in fact, independent of each other.

Information regarding the relationship between the various behaviors presumed to define the construct of impulsiveness would be of tremendous help in resolving the above issue. What needs to be done, however, would involve a rather elaborate and costly research design—a large number of individuals must agree to participate in a lengthy research project. During this period one must collect measures of their behavior in such situations as involve interpersonal influence, anxiety, shame, social norms, sensation-seeking, and so on. The intercorrelations between these various behaviors would provide an adequate test of the dimensional view. The problem here is that the subjects for such a study would have disappeared in boredom or anger before all our measures had been collected. Or the subjects would have become so "test-wise" towards the end of the data collection period, that their responses would be useless. Thus, one must be pessimistic about the possibility of conducting an adequate evaluation of either the dimensional or hierarchical view of development because of the methodological problems involved.

In a sense this is unfortunate since there are important differences between the views that personality can be described in simple linear terms as contrasted with hierarchical stages. For one thing, the hierarchical view is more idealistic. The thrust of personality development in this view is toward greater maturity, greater idealism, and greater concern with the satisfaction of higher-order needs. The dimensional view, on the other hand, makes few assumptions about the direction of growth in terms of psychological health and adjustment, with the exception of the obvious statements about the psychopathic personality. Presumably the extreme introvert may be as poorly adjusted as his opposite, the extrovert. Furthermore, personality changes that may occur over time are not attributed to an epigenesis in personality development, but to environmental or bodily events that shaped these behavioral changes. Clearly, a resolution of these two views would make a major contribution to our understanding of personality development and change.

Values and Character Structure

The next issue we wish to raise is whether impulsiveness as we have defined it is a "good" or "bad" way to be. If we listen to most personality theorists we would conclude it is "bad." Persons who do not experience anxiety or shame, who reject conventional social values, who are easily bored, and who reject advice and suggestions from others, are generally considered by diagnosticians to be psychiatrically disabled. The psychopath, for example, is described by McCord and McCord (1964) as an "asocial, aggressive, highly impulsive person, who feels little or no guilt, and is unable to form lasting bonds of affection with other human beings." (page 3).

In the same vein, those who accept a hierarchical view of personality development use many of the behaviors that are associated with impulsive-ness to define the lowest stages of personality development. The well-known stages in the development of identity described by Erikson (1959) center around such issues as feelings of shame and interpersonal trust. And as has already been mentioned, Loevinger's (1966) description of ego development defines the most primitive stages of human development in terms of impulsiveness, exploitiveness, rejection of the rules, and the like. According to this hierarchical view, the individual tends to start off poorly controlled, and self-centered, and develops through successive stages to the point where the "person proceeds beyond coping with conflict to reconciliation of con-flicting demands, and where necessary, renunciation of the unattainable, beyond toleration to the cherishing of individual differences, beyond role differentiation to the achievement of a sense of integrated identity" (Loevinger, 1966, page 200). Thus, the sequence goes from ignobility to nobility.

Let us examine how the findings from the present book fit these psychia-tric and development models. There is a partially good fit. Impulsive persons engage in what society would call maladaptive or improper behavior, that is, impulsive persons underachieved, were exploitive, had poor self-control, and were easily provoked to interpersonal aggression. They rejected conven-tional norms. On the other hand, it may be stretching a point to label as improper such behaviors as having many friends, being gregarious, revealing intimate thoughts to one's friends, maintaining independence in judgment, and not being interested in a career in the natural sciences. Furthermore, there is something positive to be said for being articulate and constructive in the classroom.

Given that neutral or even positive outcomes may be associated with impulsive behaviors, why do personality theorists generally associate these behaviors with maladaptive behavior? One possible reason has to do with the nature of the samples used in studies concerned with this question. That is, most of the conclusions reached about the prognostic significance of these core retraining behaviors are derived from studies of the psychopath and how he differs from the normal. And since the psychopath shows less control, less emotional reactivity, etc., it is easy to reach the conclusion that these "deficits" are (1) the cause of psychopathy and (2) prognostic of poor adjustment and/or developmental retardation.

If wider samples were studied, however, I believe we would more properly conclude that these behaviors differentiate persons who act in socially deviant ways from those who act conventionally. In some instances the deviancy might be expressed in nonconventional political beliefs and behavior, in other instances in nonconventional business behavior, or in nonconventional life-styles, as represented by hippie groups. And in other instances in criminal behaviors. Although this view must be considered speculative, some support can be found in Barron's research (1963) on creativity. In these well-known studies Barron compared the personalities of creative artists, writers, businessmen, mathematicians, and graduate students, with the personality of average persons in each of these respective fields. This method of criterion-grouping is similar to that used in comparing psychopaths with normals. The results of Barron's study were that creative persons appeared to have much in common with the psychopath, as customarily defined. That is, creative persons had elevated Psychopath Deviate and Manic scores on the MMPI and were poorly socialized, as measured by the Socialization Scale from the California Psychological Inventory.

Are we to conclude that creativity is a form of psychopathy or vice versa? Perhaps a more reasoned conclusion is that both creative behavior and psychopathy represent deviancy from conventional behavior. An unknown in this view concerns the reasons why this deviancy is expressed in socially unacceptable forms such as criminal acts in one instance and in innovative or creative forms in a second instance. Presumably other factors in addition to impulsiveness moderate the direction that the deviancy takes. Our point, however, is that in order for deviancy to occur in the first place, the individual may have to be somewhat restless, and not be constrained by conventional values, by anxiety or by the opinions of others. Clearly a wide range of socially deviant groups must be studied to verify this assertion.

As a final point, I find it difficult to reconcile the above view with hierarchical theories of personality development. If we accept the hierarchical view, impulsive individuals must be placed at a lower stage of development than nonimpulsive individuals. This is because impulsive persons are less accepting of conventional values, more exploitive, less controlled, and so on. Presumably the next stage in the development of impulsive individuals is for them to become nonimpulsive, whereas nonimpulsive individuals also advance, if they are not fixated at their present level. Intuitively, this kind of movement does not seem likely. From what has already been said, we would expect more interesting forms of development to be associated with the basic personality organization of impulsive persons. For instance, rejecting conventional values it could be expected that impulsive individuals might develop newer ethics, or again they might merely reject the conventional without any further additions. Conversely, we would expect nonimpulsive persons to adhere fairly closely to conventional norms throughout their lives and only to change when the majority views changed.

Conclusions

This research started with the rather practical problem of underachievement among bright adolescents. Basically we had two questions in mind at the outset—Why should impulsive individuals underachieve? What could be done about it? Underlying these questions was the value judgment of the writer that it was "bad" to underachieve, and perhaps the implicit value judgment that intelligent persons who underachieved were maladjusted persons.

As the research progressed we discovered that the act of underachievement could not be understood as an incapsulated event, but was enmeshed in the underachieving person's total way of responding to his world. It also became clear that the simple value judgments made at the beginning of the research required modification. The impulsive person revealed a variety of strengths and weaknesses, as did the nonimpulsive person. Thus, the findings have raised many new questions that were not considered initially, and for which we can now only offer speculative answers.

Nevertheless, when we review the results of the research in terms of our original purposes, we find that some of our questions have been at least partially answered. For one thing, we have a better understanding of the reasons underlying the bright impulsive individual's underachievement. In addition, we can say with some confidence that it is possible to influence the impulsive individual's level of achievement by several means. This latter finding is of interest not only for its practical implications, but also because it disabuses one of the notions that it is impossible to modify the behavior of the characterologically disturbed or extroverted personality (Eysenck, 1957). Apparently, behavior may be modified among this group if attention is paid to the nature of the incentives that are used. Our research used money as an incentive. Recently Ingram, Gerard, Quay, and Levinson (1970) used novelty and excitement with positive results, as the basis for maintaining aggressive delinquents in therapy. In both of these instances, the therapy program was designed with an appreciation of the kinds of reinforcements most appealing to impulsive persons. Perhaps the negative results generally reported in this area result from the fact that too little attention is given to the system of incentives developed to maintain these individuals in therapy.

We will close this book by noting that the issue of the role of intelligence in mediating the expression of impulsiveness remains perplexing. Simply put, the question is: Why don't less intelligent impulsive individuals behave like their more intelligent counterparts? It is my belief that the answer to this question will eventually be found in a more intensive examination of the adaptive function of intelligence during childhood. Whereas present scientific thought tends to view intellectual and personality growth as independent systems, closer examination may prove that these systems interact in critical ways to form the adult personality. This interaction presumably occurs because of the range of adaptive responses available to more and less intelligent individuals when attempting to solve problems and master their environment.

The Impulsiveness Scale

Part a.   Scoring Key

PART A. IMPULSIVENESS SCALE: SCORING KEY[a,b]

Item No.	Scored alternative	Item No.	Scored alternative
2	1	37	1, 2, 3, 4
3	1	38	1
6	1	39	1, 2
7	1	40	1, 2
9	1	41	1, 2
10	1	42	1
11	1	44	1
12	1	45	2, 3, 4
13	1	46	1, 2
14	1	47	1, 2, 3
16	1	48	1, 2, 3
18	1	49	5
20	1	50	1
21	1	51	3
22	1	52	1, 2, 3, 4
23	1	55	1
25	1		
27	1		
29	1		
30	1		
32	1		
33	1		
34	1		
35	1		
36	1		

[a] One point is given for each scored alternative.

[b] Median = 17–18;   Bottom third = 14 or less;   Top third = 21 or more.

Part b. Test Items

1.–15. When you were a boy, did you engage in the following activities
fairly often? (Answer each item separately using the following key):

    (1) Yes
    (2) No

  1. Football
  2. Diving
  3. Skiing
  4. Softball
  5. Hunting
  6. Poker
  7. Driving a motorcycle
  8. Taking care of pets

9–20. Do you remember doing the following things as a child before you
were 15? (Answer each item separately using the following key):

    (1) Yes
    (2) No

  9. Playing with snakes
10. Being interested in sex
11. Being afraid of the dark
12. Arguing with parents and teachers fairly often about your rights
13. Reading a great deal
14. Smoking
15. Playing baseball
16. Doing cruel things
17. Going on picnics with the family
18. Playing hookey
19. Eating only certain foods
20. Showing a bad temper when angry

21–31. Within the last year have you engaged in the following activities
fairly often? (Answer each item separately using the following key):

    (1) Yes
    (2) No

21. Swimming
22. Diving
23. Poker

24. Bowling
25. Auto racing
26. Bridge
27. Black Jack
28. Golf
29. Drinking parties
30. Pool
31. Tennis

32–36. Had you done the following things before you were eighteen? (Answer each item separately using the following key):

(1) Yes
(2) No

32. Hiked over 20 miles
33. Learned to swim moderately well or better
34. Learned to handle a canoe moderately well or better
35. Learned to climb mountains moderately well or better
36. Learned to walk with snow shoes

37–43. How old were you when you first did the things listed in items 37–43? (Answer each item separately using the following key):

(1) 14 or younger
(2) 15 to 16
(3) 17 to 20
(4) 21 or older
(5) Not yet

37. Meeting girls by picking them up
38. Taking an overnight trip away from home without your family
39. Dancing
40. Drinking beer
41. Drinking whiskey
42. Hitchhiking
43. Going to the library once a week or more

44. How much do you enjoy rough sports like football, boxing, wrestling, hockey?

(1) Very much
(2) Some
(3) Very little
(4) Not at all

45. In grade school, how many times a year were you sent to the principal for fooling around in class?

(1) Usually not sent
(2) Once or twice
(3) Three or four times
(4) Fairly often

46. As a boy, how frequently did you take a dare?

(1) Almost always
(2) Usually
(3) Sometimes and sometimes not
(4) Almost never
(5) Never

47. In grammar school, how frequently were you punished for bad conduct in school?

(1) Once or twice a week
(2) Almost every week
(3) Almost every month
(4) Once every year or so
(5) Rarely or never

48. How frequently has the thought entered your mind that other people dislike you or something about you?

(1) Very often
(2) Pretty regularly
(3) Occasionally
(4) Once or twice
(5) Never

49. In high school, did you help other students with their studies?

(1) Other students asked me for help with their studies
(2) Other students expected me to have ideas about what to do and how to do it
(3) Teachers asked me to explain things to other students
(4) I sought opportunities to help other students understand things
(5) I rarely helped others with their studies

50. When you are with a group of friends deciding what to do for the evening, what do you usually do?

    (1) Make a suggestion and try to get the others to accept it
    (2) Make a suggestion and let it go at that
    (3) Wait for others to make suggestions and express your opinion about their suggestions
    (4) Say nothing and go along with the others
    (5) Leave the group if you do not like the decision

51. Regardless of your income, have you managed to save anything?

    (1) I have managed to save money
    (2) I have never saved money
    (3) I have sometimes spent more than I earned

52. When you have a little extra money, which of the following do you prefer to do?

    (1) Try my luck at poker or dice
    (2) Get a good meal
    (3) Go on a date or take my wife out
    (4) Call relative or family when away from home
    (5) Save it

53–56. How often do you like to do the following when you have a free evening? (Answer each item separately using the following key):

    (1) As often as I can
    (2) Fairly often
    (3) Occasionally
    (4) Rarely

    53. Go to public dances
    54. Go to parties with a date or wife
    55. Go out with friends and stir up excitement
    56. Go to the movies

REFERENCES

Adelson, J. Personality. In P. Mussen & M. Rosenzweig (Eds.) *Annual Review of Psychology*. Palo Alto, California: Annual Reviews, Inc., 1969.

Altman, I., & Haythorn, W. W. Interpersonal exchange in isolation. *Sociometry*, 1965, **28**, 411–426.

Anderson, R. C. Educational psychology. In Paul R. Farnsworth (Ed.), *Annual Review of Psychology*. Palo Alto, California: Annual Reviews, Inc., 1967.

Barron, F. *Creativity and psychological health*. Princeton, N. J.: Van Nostrand, 1963.

Bennis, W. G., Schein, E. H., Steele, F. I., & Berlew, D. E. Interpersonal dynamics. Homewood, Ill.: The Dorsey Press, 1968.

Berkowitz, L., & Daniels, L. R. Affecting the salience of social desirability norms. *Journal of Abnormal and Social Psychology*, 1964, **65**, 275–281.

Berlyne, E. D. *Conflict, arousal and curiosity*. New York: McGraw-Hill, 1960.

Bernard, J. L., & Eisenman, R. Verbal conditioning in sociopaths with social and monetary reinforcement. *Journal of Personality and Social Psychology*, 1967, **6**, 203–206.

Bryan, J. H., & Kapche, R. Psychopathy and verbal conditioning. *Journal of Abnormal Psychology*, 1967, **72**, 71–73.

Byrne, P. Interpersonal attraction and attitude similarity. *Journal of Abnormal and Social Psychology*, 1961, **62**, 713–715.

Cairns, R. B. The influence of dependency inhibition on the effectiveness of social reinforcement. *Journal of Personality*, 1961, **29**, 466–488.

Carment, D. W., Miles, C. G. & Cervin, V. B. Persuasiveness and persuasibility as related to intelligence and extraversion. *British Journal of Social and Clinical Psychology*, 1965, **4**, 1–7.

Christie, R., & Geist, L. *Studies in Machiavellianism*. New York: Academic Press, 1970.

Clark, J. P., & Wenninger, E. P. Goal orientation and illegal behavior among juveniles. *Social Forces*, 1963, **42**, 49–59.

Cleckley, H., *The mask of sanity*. St. Louis: C. V. Mosby, 1941.

Cook, E. S., Jr. An analysis of factors related to withdrawal from high school prior to graduation. *Journal of Educational Research*, 1956, **50**, 191–196.

Dresher, R. H. Factors in voluntary dropouts. *Personal and Guidance Journal*, 1954, **32**, 287–289.

Dunnette, M. D. A modified model for test validation and selection research. *Journal of Applied Psychology*, 1963, **47**, 317–323.

Erikson, E. H. Identity and the life cycle. *Psychological Issues*, 1959, **1** (Whole No. 1).

Ewing, T. N., & Gilbert, W. M. Controlled study of the effects of counseling on the scholastic achievement of students of superior ability. *Journal of Counseling Psychology*, 1967, **14**, 235–239.

Eysenck, H. J. *The dynamics of anxiety and hysteria.* New York: Praeger, 1957.

Eysenck, H. J. *Crime and personality.* Boston: Houghton-Mifflin, 1964.

Eysenck, H. J. *The biological basis of personality.* Springfield, Ill.: Thomas, 1967.

Festinger, L. *A theory of cognitive dissonance.* New York: Harper, Row, 1957.

Festinger, L., Schachter, S. & Back, K. *Social pressures in informal groups.* New York: Harper & Bros., 1950.

Filer, R., & Meals, D. The effects of motivating conditions in the estimation of time. *Journal of Experimental Psychology*, 1949, **39**, 327–331.

Frederiksen, N., & Melville, S. D. Differential predictability in the use of test scores. *Educational and Psychological Measurement*, 1954, **14**, 647–656.

French, J. R. P., Morrison, W. H., and Levinger, G., Coercive power and forces affecting conformity. *Journal of Abnormal and Social Psychology*, 1960, **61**, 93–101.

French, J. R. P., & Raven, B. *The bases of social power.* In D. Cartwright (Ed.), *Studies in social power.* Ann Arbor, Mich.: Research Center for Group Dynamics, 1959.

Geiwitz, J. P. Hypnotically induced boredom and time estimation. *Psychonomic Science*, 1964, **9**, 277–278.

Ghiselli, E. E. Moderating effects and differential reliability and validity. *Journal of Applied Psychology*, 1963, **47**, 8–-86.

Gough, H. G. Conceptual analysis of psychological test scores and other diagnostic variables. *Journal of Abnormal Psychology*, 1965, **70**, 264–302.

Guilford, J. P. *Psychometric methods.* New York: McGraw-Hill, 1954.

Hall, C. S., & Lindzey, G. *Theories of personality.* New York: Wiley, 1957.

Hare, R. D. A conflict and learning theory analysis of psychopathic behavior. *Journal of Research in Crime and Delinquency*, 1965, **2**, 12–19.

Hare, R. D. Psychopathy, autonomic functioning and the orienting response. *Journal of Abnormal Psychology*, 1968, **73**, 1–24 (3, Pt. 2).

Harton, J. J. An investigation of the influence of success and failure on the estimation of time. *Journal of Genetic Psychology*, 1939, **21**, 51–62.

Harvey, O. J., Hunt, D. E. & Schroder, H. M. *Conceptual systems and personality organization.* New York: Wiley, 1961.

Hathaway, S. R., Reynolds, P. C., & Monachesi, E. P. Follow-up of the latter careers of 1000 boys who dropped out of high school. *Journal of Consulting and Clinical Psychology*, 1969, **33**, 370–380.

Heilbrun, A. B. Personality factors in college dropout. *Journal of Applied Psychology*, 1965, **49**, 1–7.

Hetherington, E. M., & Klinger, E. Psychopathy and punishment. *Journal of Abnormal and Social Psychology*, 1964, **69**, 113–114.

Holland, J. L. *The psychology of vocational choice: A theory of personality types and model environments.* Waltham, Mass.: Blaisdell, 1966.

Holland, J. L. Explorations of a theory of vocational choice VI. A longitudinal study using a sample of typical college students. *Journal of Applied Psychology Monograph Supplement*, 1968, **52**, 37 pp.

Ingram, G. L., Gerard, R. E., Quay, H. C., & Levinson, R. B. An experimental program for the psychopathic delinquent: Looking in the correctional waste-basket. *Journal of Research in Crime and Delinquency*, 1970, **15**, 24–30.

Jenkins, P. H. *The effects of level of character development, reward structure, and partner's role in a two-person interpersonal situation.* Ph.D. Thesis, Temple University, 1968.

Johns, J. H., & Quay, H. C. The effects of social rewards on verbal conditioning in psychopathic and neurotic military offenders. *Journal of Consulting Psychology*, 1962, **26**, 217–220.

Jourard, S. M., & Lasakow, P. Some factors in self-disclosure. *Journal of Abnormal and Social Psychology*, 1958, **56**, 91–98.

Karpman, B. The myth of the psychopathic personality. *American Journal of Psychiatry*, 1948, **104**, 523–534.

Katahn, M. Interaction of anxiety and ability in complex learning situations. *Journal of Personality and Social Psychology*, 1966, **3**, 475–478.

Kennedy, W. A., & Willcutt, H. C. Praise and blame as incentives. *Psychological Bulletin*, 1964, **62**, 323–332.

Kipnis, D. Social immaturity, intellectual ability and adjustive behavior in college. *Journal of Applied Psychology*, 1968, **52**, 71–80 (b).

Kipnis, D. Intelligence as a modifier of the behavior of character disorders. *Journal of Applied Psychology*, 1965, **49**, 237–242 (a).

Kipnis, D. The relationship between persistence, insolence, and performance as a function of general ability. *Educational and Psychological Measurement*, 1965, **25**, 95–110.

Kipnis, D. A non-cognitive correlate of performance among lower aptitude men. *Journal of Applied Psychology*, 1962, **46**, 76–80.

Kipnis, D., & Wagner, C. The interaction of personality and intelligence in task performance. *Educational and Psychological Measurement*, 1965, **25**, 731–744. (a)

Kipnis, D., & Wagner, C. Effects of motivation to strive on personality-perform-ance relationships. *Journal of Experimental Research in Personality*, 1965, **1**, 138–143. (b)

Kipnis, D., & Glickman, A. S. The prediction of job performance. *Journal of Applied Psychology*, 1962, **46**, 50–56.

Kipnis, D. M. Changes in self-concept in relation to perception of others. *Journal of Personality*, 1961, **29**, 449–465.

Kogan, N., & Tagiuri, R. Interpersonal preference and cognitive organization. *Journal of Abnormal and Social Psychology*, 1958, **56**, 113–116.

Lazovik, A. D., & Lang, P. J. A laboratory demonstration of systematic desensi-tization psychotherapy. *Journal of Psychological Studies*, 1960, **11**, 238–247.

Levine, M., & Spivack, G. Incentive time conception and self control in a group of emotionally disturbed boys. *Journal of Clinical Psychology*, 1959, **15**, 110–113.

Loevinger, J. The meaning and measurement of ego development. *American Psychologist*, 1966, **21**, 195–206.

Lykken, D. T. A study of anxiety in the sociopathic personality. *Journal of Abnormal and Social Psychology*, 1957, **55**, 6–10.

Lynd, Helen M. *On shame and the search for identity.* New York: Science Editions, 1958.

McClelland, D. C., & Winter, D. G. *Motivating economic achievement.* New York: The Free Press, 1969.

McCord, W., & McCord, J. *The psychopath: An essay on the criminal mind.* Princeton, N. J.: Van Nostrand, 1964.

McCord, W., McCord, J., & Zola, I. K. *Origins of crime.* New York: Columbia University Press, 1959.

Mead, M. *From the South Seas.* New York: Morrow, 1939.

Miller, N. E. Studies of fear as an acquirable drive. *Journal of Experimental Psychology,* 1948, **38**, 89–101.

Mowrer, O. H. A stimulus-response analysis of anxiety. *Psychological Review,* 1939, **46**, 553–565.

Newcomb, T. M. *The acquaintance process.* New York: Holt, Rinehart and Winston, 1961.

Orme, J. E. Time estimation and personality. *Journal of Mental Science,* 1962, **108**, 213–216.

Panton, J. H. MMPI Code Configurations as related to measures of intelligence among a state prison population. *Journal of Social Psychology,* 1960, **51**, 403–407.

Persons, R. W. Verbal operant conditioning of severely antisocial adolescents by delinquent and normal E's. *Psychological Report,* 1968, **22**, 745–748.

Quay, H. C. Psychopathic personality as pathological stimulation seeking. *American Journal of Psychiatry,* 1965, **122**, 180–183.

Roethlisberger, F. J., Dickson, W. J., & Wright, H. A. *Management and the workers.* Cambridge, Mass.: Harvard University Press, 1949.

Roessel, F. P. Minnesota Multiphasic Personality Inventory results for high school dropouts and graduates. *Dissertation Abstracts,* 1954, **14**, 942–943.

Rotter, J. B. Generalized expectancies for internal versus external control of reinforcement. *Psychological Monographs,* 1966, **80**, 28 p.

Sarbin, T. R., Allen, V. L., & Rutherford, E. E. Social reinforcement, socialization and chronic delinquency. *British Journal of Social and Clinical Psychology,* 1965, **4**, 179–184.

Saunders, D. R. Moderator variables in prediction. *Educational and Psychological Measurement,* 1965, **16**, 209–222.

Schmauk, F. J. *A study of the relationship between kinds of punishment, autonomic arousal, subjective anxiety and avoidance learning in the primary sociopath.* Ph.D. thesis, Temple University Graduate School, April, 1968.

Schwitzgebel, R. L. Preliminary socialization for psychotherapy of behavior-disordered adolescents. *Journal of Consulting and Clinical Psychology,* 1969, **33**, 71–77.

Siegman, A. W. The relation between future time perspective, time estimation, and impulse control in a group of young offenders and in a control group. *Journal of Consulting Psychology,* 1961, **25**, 470–475.

Simpkins, Ruth E. *Verbal performance effected by social maturity and social and material incentives.* Ph.D. Thesis, Temple University, 1968.

Stagner, R. The relation of personality to academic aptitude and achievement. *Journal of Educational Research,* 1933, **26**, 648–660.

Spielberger, C. D., Denny, J. P., & Weitz, H. The effects of group counseling on the academic performance of anxious college freshmen. *Journal of Counseling Psychology,* 1962, **9**, 195–204.

Stewart, D. J., & Resnick, J. H. Verbal conditioning and dependency behavior in delinquents. *Journal of Abnormal Psychology* (in press).

Stewart, D. J., & Resnick, J. H. Verbal conditioning of psychopaths as a function of experimenter-sex differences. *Journal of Abnormal Psychology,* 1970, **75,** 90–92.

Sullivan, C., Grant, M. Q., & Grant, J. D. The development of interpersonal maturity. *Psychiatry,* 1957, **20,** 373–385.

Super, D. E. *The psychology of careers.* New York: Harper, 1957.

Swingle, P. G. *Experiments in social psychology.* New York: Academic Press, 1968.

Taffel, C. Anxiety and the conditioning of verbal behavior. *Journal of Abnormal and Social Psychology,* 1955, **51,** 496–501.

Taylor, D. A., & Altman, I. *Intimacy-scaled stimuli for use in studies of interpersonal relations.* (Research Rep. No. 9) Bethesda, Md., Naval Medical Research Institute, 1966.

Taylor, F. W. *The principles of scientific management.* New York: Harper, 1911.

Thorne, F. C. The etiology of sociopathic reactions. *American Journal of Psychotherapy,* 1959, **15,** 110–113.

Torrance, E. P., & Ziller, R. C. *Risk and life experience: Development of a scale for measuring risk-taking tendencies.* (Tech. Rep. No. 57–23), United States Air Force, Washington Air Defense Center, 1957.

Tyler, V. O. Exploring the use of operant techniques in the rehabilitation of delinquent boys. Paper presented at the meeting of the American Psychological Association Meetings, Fall, 1965.

Wheeler, L. Toward a theory of behavioral contagion. *Psychological Review,* 1966, **73,** 179–192.

Wheeler, L. & Caggiula, A. R. The contagion of aggression. *Journal of Experimental Social Psychology,* 1966, **2,** 1–10.

Wright, P. H. A model and a technique for studies of friendship. *Journal of Experimental Social Psychology,* 1969, **5,** 295–309.

Vroom, V. H. *Work and motivation.* New York: Wiley, 1964.

Zajonic, R. B. Social facilitation. *Science,* 1965, **149,** 269–274.

Zipf, S. G. Resistance and conformity under reward and punishment. *Journal of Abnormal and Social Psychology,* 1960, **61,** 102–109.

Zubeck, J. P. *Sensory deprivation: Fifteen years of research.* New York: Appleton-Century-Crofts, 1969.

Zuckerman, M., Kolin, E. A., Price, L., & Zoob, I. Development of a Sensation-Seeking Scale. *Journal of Consulting Psychology,* 1964, **28,** 477–482.

Zuckerman, M., & Link, K. Construct validity for the Sensation-Seeking Scale. *Journal of Consulting and Clinical Psychology,* 1968, **32,** 420–426.

Author Index

Numbers in Italics refer to the pages on which the complete references are listed.

A

Adelson, J., *124*
Allen, V. L., 7, 99, *127*
Altman, I., 65, 69, 71, *124, 128*
Anderson, R. C., 110, *124*

B

Back, K., 68, *125*
Barron, F., 96, 116, *124*
Bennis, W. G., 72, *124*
Berkowitz, L., 76, *124*
Berlew, D. E., 72, *124*
Berlyne, E. D., 4, 5, *124*
Bernard, J. L., 7, *124*
Bryan, J. H., 7, *124*
Byrne, P., 71, *124*

C

Caggiula, A. R., 49, *128*
Cairns, R. B., 7, 99, *124*
Carment, D. W., 26, *124*
Cervin, V. B., 26, *124*
Christie, R., 110, *124*
Clark, J. P., 30, *124*
Cleckley, H., 4, 58, *124*
Cook, Jr., E. S., 23, *124*

D

Daniels, L. R., 76, *124*
Denny, J. P., 98, 110, *127*
Dickson, W. J., 57, *127*
Dresher, R. H., 23, *124*
Dunnette, M. D., 19, *124*

E

Eisenman, R., 7, *124*
Erikson, E. H., 115, *124*
Ewing, T. N., 110, *125*
Eysenck, H. J., 4, 6, 34, 58, 72, 112, 113, 117, *125*

F

Festinger, L., 60, 68, *125*
Filer, R., 34, *125*
Frederiksen, N., 19, *125*
French, J. R. P., 34, 51, *125*

G

Geist, L., 112, *124*
Geiwitz, J. P., 34, *125*
Gerard, R. E., 117, *125*
Ghiselli, E. E., 19, *125*
Gilbert, W. M., 110, *125*
Glickman, A. S., 13, 19, *126*
Goodstadt, B. E., 80, *125*
Gough, H. G., 26, 112, *125*
Grant, J. D., 113, *127*
Grant, M. Q., 113, *127*
Guilford, J. P., 68, 71, *125*

H

Hall, C. S., 1, *125*
Hare, R. D., 5, 6, 36, *125*
Harton, J. J., 34, *125*
Harvey, O. J., 30, *125*
Hathaway, S. R., 22, *125*
Haythorn, W. W., 65, 69, 71, *124*

129

Subject Index

Date Due

VA

Hino

The Story of VAMPIRE KNIGHT

1 Cross Academy, a private boarding school, is where the Day Class and the Night Class coexist. The Night Class—a group of beautiful elite students—are all vampires!

2 Four years ago, after turning his twin brother Ichiru against him, the pureblood Shizuka Hio bit Zero and turned him into a vampire. Kaname kills Shizuka, but the source may still exist. Meanwhile, Yuki suffers from lost memories. When Kaname sinks his fangs into her neck, her memories return!

3 Yuki is the princess of the Kuran family—and a pureblood vampire!! Ten years ago, her mother exchanged her life to seal away Yuki's vampire nature. Yuki's Uncle Rido killed her father. Rido takes over Shiki's body and arrives at the Academy. He targets Yuki for her blood, so Kaname gives his own blood to resurrect Rido. Kaname confesses that he is the progenitor of the Kurans, and that Rido is the master who awakened him!

NIGHT CLASS

DAY CLASS

She adores him.

He saved her 10 years ago.

Childhood Friends

KANAME KURAN

Night Class President and pureblood vampire. Yuki adores him. He's the progenitor of the Kurans...!!

YUKI CROSS

The heroine. The adopted daughter of the Headmaster, and a Guardian who protects Cross Academy. She is a princess of the Kuran family.

Foster Father

ZERO KIRYU

Yuki's childhood friend, and a Guardian. Shizuka turned him into a vampire. He will eventually lose his sanity, falling to Level E.

COUSINS

HANABUSA AIDO
Nickname: Idol

AKATSUKI KAIN
Nickname: Wild

TAKUMA ICHIJO
Night Class Vice President. He has been kidnapped by Sara, a pureblood.

HEADMASTER CROSS
He raised Yuki. He hopes to educate those who will become a bridge between humans and vampires. He used to be a skilled hunter.

RIDO KURAN

Yuki's uncle. He caused Yuki's parents to die, and Kaname shattered his body, but he resurrected after 10 years. He tried to obtain Yuki, but Yuki and Zero killed him.

ICHIRU

Zero's younger twin brother. He gave his blood to Zero to turn him into the strongest hunter.

SARA SHIRABUKI
A pureblood. She killed the pureblood Ouri to obtain his power, and has turned human girls into vampires. She claims she wants to become a "Queen," but what does she mean?!

*Purebloods are vampires who do not have a single drop of human blood in their lineage. They are very powerful, and they can turn humans into vampires by drinking their blood.

4 Cross Academy turns into a battlefield. After fierce fighting, Yuki and Zero succeed in defeating Rido, but then Zero points his gun at Yuki. No matter what their feelings are, their fates will never intertwine. Yuki leaves the Academy with Kaname, and the Night Class at Cross Academy is no more.

5 A year has passed since Yuki and Zero's parting. Kaname and Zero have become the representatives of each group respectively. Sara Shirabuki begins making suspicious moves by creating more servants of her own. Kaname gives Yuki his blood to show her his memories of the time the progenitors existed. Yuki sees a woman with whom Kaname shared a strong bond in the past. Distressed at how vampires were preying on humans, the woman gave up her life to cast her heart into a furnace, creating weapons humans could use to kill vampires. The resulting substance became the base of vampire hunter weapons.

6 Kaname has continued on since the age of the progenitors with darkness and longing in his heart. Yuki makes the decision to stay with Kaname, but he disappears right after beheading Aido's father. Now Yuki has been taken into custody by the Hunter Society?!

VAMPIRE KNIGHT

Contents

VAMPIRE KNIGHT

SIXTY-NINTH NIGHT: I AM YUKI KURAN

FOLLOW
ME.

IT'S
THIS
WAY.

Hino here. Thank you very much for purchasing this volume! The series has finally reached volume 15. I'm sure there are those who have recently started reading this series as well as those who have been following it for a long time. I'm also sure there are others out there who rarely follow this series now. Now that there are 15 volumes, I can say this manga would not have continued this long without your support. I can feel my blood burning passionately with gratitude for you all. Thank you very much! I have been a mangaka for 17 years now, and I am still inadequate, But I promise to put all my effort into this work. I wrote an 8-page bonus story for this volume, so I hope you enjoy it...!

TMP TMP

FINAP

FINAP

FATHER!

MOTHER!

IT'S NICE TO SEE YOU LIVELY, BUT...

WHAT IS IT, MARIA?

IT'S KANAME-SAMA.

THE HEAD OF KURAN HAS GONE MISSING.

I'M SORRY.

I USED THE BIRD'S EYES AND EARS TO EAVESDROP ON THE NOBLES.

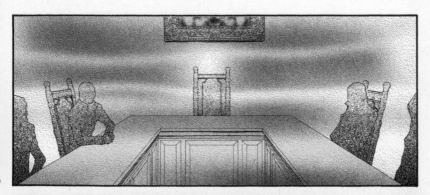

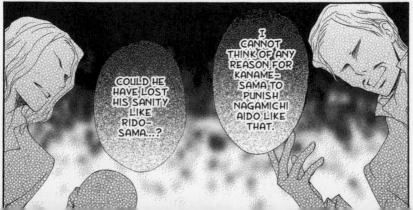

I CANNOT THINK OF ANY REASON FOR KANAME-SAMA TO PUNISH NAGAMICHI AIDO LIKE THAT.

COULD HE HAVE LOST HIS SANITY LIKE RIDO-SAMA...?

I KNOW.

...THE
MEMORIES
OF THIS
LITTLE
GIRL?

I WANT VAMPIRES AND HUMANS...

...TO GET ALONG PEACE-FULLY.

I PROMISE I'LL COME FIND YOU, KANAME.

IN THAT CASE, YOU CAN GO.

HEY...

OKAY.

SO FOR NOW...

BOW

...I MUST...

..DO WHAT I HAVE TO.

DASH

SIXTY-NINTH NIGHT/END

SOB
SOB
SOB

I HIT HER AND SAID MEAN THINGS TO HER... AND... AND...

IT'S OVER... YUKKIE WON'T LIKE ME ANY- MORE.

DON'T WORRY. SHE NEVER LIKED YOU THAT MUCH TO BEGIN WITH.

YUKKIE AND I HAVE BEEN CLOSE FOR TEN YEARS...

THAT'S NOT TRUE!!

SHUT UP! IT WASN'T BECAUSE SHE DISLIKED ME OR ANYTHING !!

EVEN AFTER ALL THOSE YEARS...

THEN I WONDER WHY SHE WON'T CALL YOU "FATHER."

VAMPIRE KNIGHT

SEVENTIETH NIGHT:
COOPERATORS

SEVENTIETH NIGHT/END

VAMPIRE KNIGHT

SEVENTY-FIRST NIGHT:
THE NEW NIGHT CLASS

IT HAS BEEN OVER A YEAR SINCE THAT BUILDING COLLAPSED, THEREFORE...

IT WILL BE CALLED THE "NIGHT CLASS."

I DON'T REMEMBER MUCH ABOUT IT.

ISN'T IT? I THINK.

THE NIGHT CLASS IS FOR THE SMART STUDENTS, RIGHT?

BUT...

...IT'S STRANGE, ISN'T IT?

I ASKED MR. YAGARI, SO I'M POSITIVE.

AH! I'M SO HAPPY...

REALLY?!

AIDO'S COMING BACK TOO?!

...PLEASE FEEL FREE...

...TO USE ME AS YOUR **ERRAND GIRL!**

NO, FOOL!

...OR "PLEASE TALK TO ME," YOU STUPID PURE-BLOOD!

YOU SHOULD HAVE SAID, "PLEASE FOLLOW MY EXAMPLE"...

WHY ARE YOU UPSET?

I SHOULDN'T HAVE SAID THAT?

SILENCE

YOU DON'T AGREE...?

UM...

I MEANT WHAT I SAID! WE HAVE TO GET ALONG AS FRIENDS FROM NOW ON...

...EVERY-ONE!

AAAH, THERE GOES THE PRESTIGE OF THE PURE-BLOODS...

WHAT IS IT?

SEVENTY-FIRST NIGHT/END

VAMPIRE KNIGHT

SEVENTY-SECOND NIGHT: THE TASTE OF TABLETS

AND I CAN'T GO BACK...

...TO BEING HUMAN.

I WOULD HAVE COME TO GREET YOU ALL, YOU KNOW.

THANK YOU, TAKUMA.

THP

YOU'RE STARVING, AREN'T YOU?

TABLETS...

...ARE SYNTHETIC SUBSTANCES CULTURED FROM VARIOUS TYPES OF BLOOD-FORMING CELLS.

I...

...DO NOT KNOW FROM WHOSE BLOOD CELLS THESE CAME...

HOW VERY SAD.

VAMPIRE KNIGHT

SEVENTY-THIRD NIGHT:
MY RELATIONSHIP WITH ZERO

YOUR REACTION TIME IS SLOW.

YOU JUST LET A VAMPIRE WALK RIGHT UP TO YOU.

Many thanks!

O. Mio-sama
K. Midori-sama
I. Asami-sama
A. Ichiya-sama
And to my family, friends, and the people all around me... I'd like to apologize to my editor and all the people for whom I've caused trouble. And thanks to all the readers too.

Thank you very much. I would not have been able to get this far if even a few of those people had not been around, so I would like to thank you all from the bottom of my heart.

It seems that volume 16 will be published in five months. I hope you will continue to follow this series when it comes out. I'll put all my effort into it...!!!

Matsuri Hino

Over and out.

I update only once in a while, but the address of my blog has changed.

http://hino-matsuri.jugem.jp/

I HAVE TO PULL MYSELF TOGETHER...

...OR ELSE REESTAB-LISHING THE NIGHT CLASS WILL BE MEANING-LESS...

...ALONG WITH MY VOWS TO PURSUE KANAME...

IT'S STILL CON-NECTED TO ZERO.

IF I AM TO LET YOU GO...

...I'D RATHER KILL YOU MYSELF OR HAVE YOU KILL ME...

KANAME FORGAVE MY WORDS AND ALLOWED ME TO BE WITH HIM...

...AND TO KEEP RUN-NING FROM ZERO.

IT'S THE WAY WE'VE ALWAYS BEEN TOGETHER...

...ZERO.

SEVENTY-THIRD NIGHT/END

SECRETS

HE TOLD YOU HE WAS THE PROGENITOR, DIDN'T HE?

HE TOLD YOU EVERYTHING ABOUT HIMSELF, DIDN'T HE?

THE MAN WHO KNOWS KANAME'S SECRETS.

TAKUMA ICHIJO.

TELL ME HIS WEAK-NESSES.

I KNOW ALL ABOUT HIM.

MAKE ME FEEL HAPPY.

I DO.

SO YOU WANT TO HEAR THEM?

I'LL TELL YOU ABOUT THE TIME WHEN YUKI ENTERED HIGH SCHOOL.

VERY WELL...

SHE HAD SUCH LONG, PRETTY HAIR...

...BUT SHE CUT IT, YOU KNOW...

YUKI CUT HER HAIR?

WHAT'S IT LIKE NOW?

SKRTCH

SKRTCH

TUP

...

KANAME... YOU...

I WAS THE ONE WHO KNOCKED AIDO UNCON-SCIOUS...

...THOUGH HE HAD DONE NOTHING WRONG.

WHAT IS IT? WHAT IS IT?

BACK WHEN A STUDENT IN YUKI'S CLASS HAD A CRUSH ON HER...

HOW AMUSING. I AM FAR BETTER THAN HE IS.

TEE HEE HEE

I THOUGHT I HAD TO HIDE THE TRUTH...

NEXT.

PUDDING! PUDDING!

B-BMP

B-BMP

VVSH

CR...

CROSS...!

TO MISS YUKI CROSS

YOU DESIRE TO CONTINUE LIVING?

THEN DON'T GO NEAR HER AGAIN...

KRSS KRSS

STOP THAT, KANAME. WHAT DO YOU THINK YOU'RE DOING?

RRIP

THOSE ARE...

...WEAKNESSES?

SHUMP SHUMP

WHAT? WHAT?

HOW BORING.

NEXT.

SECRETS/END

EDITOR'S NOTES

Characters

Matsuri Hino puts careful thought into the names of her characters in *Vampire Knight*. Below is the collection of characters through volume 15. Each character's name is presented family name first, per the kanji reading.

黒主優姫

Cross Yuki

Yuki's last name, *Kurosu*, is the Japanese pronunciation of the English word "cross." However, the kanji has a different meaning—*kuro* means "black" and *su* means "master." Her first name is a combination of *yuu*, meaning "tender" or "kind," and *ki*, meaning "princess."

錐生零

Kiryu Zero

Zero's first name is the kanji for *rei*, meaning "zero." In his last name, *Kiryu*, the *ki* means "auger" or "drill," and the *ryu* means "life."

玖蘭枢

Kuran Kaname

Kaname means "hinge" or "door." The kanji for his last name is a combination of the old-fashioned way of writing *ku*, meaning "nine," and *ran*, meaning "orchid": "nine orchids."

藍堂英

Aido Hanabusa

Hanabusa means "petals of a flower." *Aido* means "indigo temple." In Japanese, the pronunciation of *Aido* is very close to the pronunciation of the English word *idol*.

架院暁

Kain Akatsuki

Akatsuki means "dawn" or "daybreak." In *Kain, ka* is a base or support, while *in* denotes a building that has high fences around it, such as a temple or school.

早園瑠佳

Souen Ruka

In *Ruka*, the *ru* means "lapis lazuli" while the *ka* means "good-looking" or "beautiful." The *sou* in Ruka's surname, *Souen*, means "early," but this kanji also has an obscure meaning of "strong fragrance." The *en* means "garden."

一条拓麻

Ichijo Takuma

Ichijo can mean a "ray" or "streak." The kanji for *Takuma* is a combination of *taku*, meaning "to cultivate" and *ma*, which is the kanji for *asa*, meaning "hemp" or "flax," a plant with blue flowers.

支葵千里

Shiki Senri

Shiki's last name is a combination of *shi*, meaning "to support" and *ki*, meaning "mallow"—a flowering plant with pink or white blossoms. The *ri* in *Senri* is a traditional Japanese unit of measure for distance, and one *ri* is about 2.44 miles. *Senri* means "1,000 *ri*."

夜刈十牙
Yagari Toga
Yagari is a combination of *ya*, meaning
"night," and *gari*, meaning "to harvest."
Toga means "ten fangs."

一条麻遠，一翁
Ichijo Asato, aka "Ichio"
Ichijo can mean a "ray" or "streak."
Asato's first name is comprised of *asa*,
meaning "hemp" or "flax," and *tou*,
meaning "far off." His nickname is *ichi*,
or "one," combined with *ou*, which can
be used as an honorific when referring
to an older man.

若葉沙頼
Wakaba Sayori
Yori's full name is Sayori Wakaba.
Wakaba means "young leaves." Her
given name, *Sayori*, is a combination of *sa*, meaning "sand," and
yori, meaning "trust."

星煉
Seiren

Sei means "star" and *ren* means "to smelt" or "refine." *Ren* is also the same kanji used in *rengoku*, or "purgatory."

遠矢莉磨
Toya Rima

Toya means a "far-reaching arrow." Rima's first name is a combination of *ri*, or "jasmine," and *ma*, which signifies enhancement by wearing away, such as by polishing or scouring.

紅まり亜
Kurenai Maria

Kurenai means "crimson." The kanji for the last *a* in Maria's first name is the same that is used in "Asia."

錐生壱縷
Kiryu Ichiru

Ichi is the old-fashioned way of writing "one," and *ru* means "thread."

緋桜閑, 狂咲姫
Hio Shizuka, Kuruizaki-hime

Shizuka means "calm and quiet." In Shizuka's family name, *hi* is "scarlet," and *ou* is "cherry blossoms." Shizuka Hio is also referred to as the "Kuruizaki-hime." *Kuruizaki* means "flowers blooming out of season," and *hime* means "princess."

藍堂月子
Aido Tsukiko

Aido means "indigo temple." *Tsukiko* means "moon child."

白蕗更
Shirabuki Sara

Shira is "white," and *buki* is "butterbur," a plant with white flowers. *Sara* means "renew."

黒主灰閻
Cross Kaien

Cross, or *Kurosu*, means "black master." Kaien is a combination of *kai*, meaning "ashes," and *en*, meaning "village gate." The kanji for *en* is also used for Enma, the ruler of the Underworld in Buddhist mythology.

玖蘭李土
Kuran Rido

Kuran means "nine orchids." In *Rido*, *ri* means "plum" and *do* means "earth."

玖蘭樹里

Kuran Juri

Kuran means "nine orchids." In her first name, *ju* means "tree" and a *ri* is a traditional Japanese unit of measure for distance. The kanji for *ri* is the same as in Senri's name.

玖蘭悠

Kuran Haruka

Kuran means "nine orchids." *Haruka* means "distant" or "remote."

鷹宮海斗

Takamiya Kaito

Taka means "hawk" and *miya* means "imperial palace" or "shrine." *Kai* is "sea" and *to* means "to measure" or "grid."

菖藤依砂也

Shoto Isaya

Sho means "Siberian Iris" and *to* is "wisteria." The *I* in *Isaya* means "to rely on," while the *sa* means "sand." *Ya* is a suffix used for emphasis.

橙茉

Toma

In the family name *Toma*, *to* means "seville orange" and *ma* means "jasmine flower."

藍堂永路

Aido Nagamichi

The name *Nagamichi* is a combination of *naga*, which means "long" or "eternal," and *michi*, which is the kanji for "road" or "path." *Aido* means "indigo temple."

縹木

Hanadagi

In this family name, *Hanada* means "bright light blue" and *gi* means "tree."

Terms

-sama: The suffix *sama* is used in formal address for someone who ranks higher in the social hierarchy. The vampires call their leader "Kaname-sama" only when they are among their own kind.

Matsuri Hino burst onto the manga scene with her series *Kono Yume ga Sametara* (When This Dream Is Over), which was published in *LaLa DX* magazine. Hino was a manga artist a mere nine months after she decided to become one.

With the success of her popular series *Captive Hearts* and *MeruPuri*, Hino has established herself as a major player in the world of shojo manga. *Vampire Knight* is currently serialized in *LaLa* magazine.

Hino enjoys creative activities and has commented that she would have been either an architect or an apprentice to traditional Japanese craft masters if she had not become a manga artist.

SURPRISE!

You may be reading the wrong way!

It's true: In keeping with the original Japanese comic format, this book reads from right to left—so action, sound effects, and word balloons are completely reversed. This preserves the orientation of the original artwork—plus, it's fun! Check out the diagram shown here to get the hang of things, and then turn to the other side of the book to get started!